Contemporary Works in Economic Sciences
Legal Informatics, Economics, OR and Mathematics

Contemporary Works in Economic Sciences
Legal Informatics, Economics, OR and Mathematics

Edited by
Munenori Kitahara
Hiroaki Teramoto
Hiroshima Shudo University

Volume 7 in a Series of Monographs of Contemporary Social Systems Solutions
Produced by the Faculty of Economic Sciences, Hiroshima Shudo University

Kyushu University Press

Volume 7 in a Series of Monographs of Contemporary Social Systems Solutions
Produced by Hiroshima Shudo University

All rights reserved. No part of this publication may be reproduced or transmitted in any form or by any means, electronic or mechanical, including photocopying and recording, or by any information storage and retrieval system, without the written permission from the publisher.

Copyright © 2016 by Munenori Kitahara and Hiroaki Teramoto
3-8-34-305, Momochihama, Sawara-ku, Fukuoka-shi, 814-0001, Japan

ISBN978-4-7985-0179-6

Printed in Japan

Preface

Hiroshima Shudo University established the Faculty of Economic Sciences in 1977 and the Graduate School of Economic Sciences in 2001. One goal of this faculty is to unify information sciences and economics and the faculty has endeavored to make progress in the research fields of operations research, computer sciences, mathematical economics and econometrics. While the definition of economic sciences has not been established yet, our specific understanding is that the economic sciences should unite system sciences and qualitative economic analysis and construct new fields relating to the management of the international economy, the financial system, and the national economy, or environmental issues, legal policies in communication.

The Faculty of Economic Sciences is a unique academic institution. There are no other faculties titled as "economic sciences" in Japan. Basically, we pursue analyzing various issues of contemporary economies and social systems, but its uniqueness can be observed in our efforts to balance the traditional economics and information sciences as means of analytical tools.

The Faculty consists of some 30 highly qualified members, whose research interests span a wide range of topics but more or less concern quantitative analytical frameworks. Since 2005 we have been publishing our research results in a form of monographs in English, one or two volumes a year, in order to present our academic contributions to possible readers in the world.

In the past several years, members of this faculty have made plans to expand these new frontiers as follows:
1. Macro-econometric models or micro-models which contain international economics or micro-models.
2. System analysis of financial institutions and international trade.
3. Information sciences, such as network systems or information systems or theory of reliance.
4. System sciences, such as operations research and production system analysis.
5. Research on information society and social systems.
6. Legal informatics, applying information technology to legal fields and solution of legal problems in digital society.

Faculty members have undertaken joint research with the aim of constructing these new fields and to publish our new research as a monograph as follows:

Quantitative Economic Analysis, International Trade and Finance (2005)

Applied Economic Informatics and Systems Sciences (2005)

Quantitative Analysis of Modern Economy (2007)
System Sciences for Economics and Informatics (2007)
Quantitative Analysis on Contemporary Economic Issues (2008)
Research on Information Society and Social Systems (2008)
Social Systems Solutions by Legal Informatics, Economic Sciences and Computer Sciences (2009)
The New Viewpoints and New Solutions of Economic Sciences in the Information Society (2010)
Social Systems Solutions Applied by Economic Sciences and Mathematical Solutions (2011)
Social Systems Solutions through Economic Sciences (2012)
Legal Informatics, Economic Science and Mathematical Research (2013)
New Solutions in Legal Informatics, Economic Sciences and Mathematics (2014)

In these monographs our aim is to develop new methods and materials for constructing new fields of economics.

The authors of papers in these monographs have participate in building this new faculty and worked to develop new horizons of system sciences, information sciences, economics, economic sciences, computer sciences and legal informatics. We would welcome comments or suggestions in any forms.

The 2015 monograph is also entirely financed by the Faculty of Economic Sciences and is entitled under the title of "Contemporary Works in Economic Sciences" edited by Munenori Kitahara and Hiroaki Teramoto.

This book contains contributions from wide variety of research in information society, information sciences, economic sciences, systems approach to the economic, managerial, mathematical and legal subjects. The focus of most articles is on the recent developments in the relevant. The set of papers in this book reflect both each theory and wide range of applications to economic and managerial models. The economic sciences is based upon an interdisciplinary education and research area of sciences economics, econometrics, statistics, information sciences, system sciences, application information sciences, operations research and legal informatics.

This book consists of six chapters as follows:

Chapter 1, by *Munenori Kitahara*, refers to an audit for compliance in an electronic commerce. Legal states would require the residents and the entities of both lawful individual behaviors and business activities. The residents could receive online administrative, financial, commercial and educational services from the Web 24/7 on the Internet or the Cloud. It goes without saying that the entities have been developed the enterprises on the based upon the hi-powered information processing systems on the Internet or the Cloud.

Therefore, the systems should guarantee both the legality of behaviors and the compliance of enterprises. That is a problem of system architecture. That is, the systems have to be equipped with an architecture which can guarantee the legality and the compliance.

The architecture can be defined based on the ideas of "privacy by design," "security by default," and "IAM (identity and access management)." The concept is that the various requirements of laws, regulations and policies could be reached by an engineering method. That is, the systems would be designed upon those requirements. In other words, the requirements would be embedded into the architecture of systems.

To protect system, application, and information from internal and external threats and to comply with various regulatory, privacy and data protection requirements, organizations implement industry standard frameworks. IAM is as much an aspect of architecture as it is a collection of information technology components processes, and standard practices. As much as cloud IAM architecture and practices impact the efficiency of internal IT processes, they also play a major role in managing compliance within the enterprise.

There are left some unsolved problems. The one is a relationship between law and information technology. In fact, information technologies would control human's behaviors in spite of human's intention. The other is that whether it is right or not, that legal justice would be maintained by information technologies.

Chapter 2, by *Chris Czerkawski and Osamu Kurihara*, will deal with the macroeconomic policies of the present prime minister. That is, this chapter is on macroeconomic policies known as Abenomics implemented in Japanese economy under so-called three arrows policy. The paper summarizes the nature of Japanese economic crisis, the instruments implemented to foster economic growth and stimulate demand, the empirical consequences of the measures applied in the last ten years. The effectiveness of these measures is discussed in context of economic theories of crisis, the empirical results confirmed by statistics and in international comparative context. The failures and shortcomings of these policies are presented and conclusions drawn on existing potential for resolving the crisis.

Chapter 3, by *Hiroaki Teramoto* will research on health economics. This chapter introduces and considers three representative articles on health economics, particularly medical expenditure. A consumer's behavior is affected by his or her level of health. If one's health declines (illness), the consumer changes his or her behavior. In industrialized countries or aging societies, overall expenditure for medical care is increasing and becoming an imminent problem. The field of economics has a significant amount of research on this field, some of which was reviewed for this study. The first two studies on cost-effective analysis were by Garber and Phelps, and Meltzer. The third study is the work of Graff Zivin and Neidell, who analyzed the effects of medical care when environmental pollution occurs. These three works depend on the consumer's (expected) utility maximization. The author believes that these three studies are pioneering in their field and deserve introduction and consideration.

Chapter 4, by *Nan Zhang* will examine the theoretical framework of global flow of funds. The main purpose of this chapter is a trial to measure Global Flow of Funds (GFF), it includes four portions. Firstly, the paper will give a definition on GFF, based on the definition to decide the statistical domains of GFF, and build a statistical monitoring system for GFF using economic concepts and theoretical frameworks. Secondly, the paper sets out the concepts and existing data sources and integrates the data sources for measure GFF which are reflected in the Balance of Payments, International Investment Position (IIP), the Coordinated Direct Investment Survey (CDIS), the Coordinated Portfolio Investment Survey (CPIS), Consolidated Banking Statistics (CBS), and in the "rest-of-the-world" account of the national accounts. These datasets provide valuable information for the analysis of GFF. Thirdly, The Balance Sheet Approach is used to break down the rest of the world by components of IIP. An external statistics' matrix (metadata) exercise shows what external sector financial data are available by IIP concept. As the outcome of the study, this paper compiled Global Flow of Find Matrix with the pattern of "Country by Country" matrix. Fourthly, as well as an example illustrating how the GFF matrix operates.

Chapter 5, by *Setsuko Sakai and Tetsuyuki Takahama* will research on detecting ridge structure for population-based optimization algorithms. There exist many studies on solving optimization problems using population-based optimization algorithms (POAs). POAs such as evolutionary algorithms have been proved to be powerful function optimization algorithms and outperform conventional optimization algorithms. However, there exist some difficult optimization problems such as problems with ridge structure. In problems with ridge structure, search points will move through a narrow path to find better points, the diversity of search points will be lost, and the search process will be slowed down or even be stopped at a local solution. If ridge structure can be detected, the efficiency and robustness of the search process can be improved by selecting proper algorithm parameters to keep the diversity. In this study, we propose three methods of detecting ridge structure and also propose a method of controlling algorithm parameters adaptively for ridge structure. The performances of the methods are compared by optimizing several functions with controlling algorithm parameters.

Chapter 6, by *Ryoko Wada* and *Yoshio Agaoka* will deal with harmonic polynomials of more degree. Concerning classical harmonic polynomials on $\mathbf{C}^p$, many results have been obtained from several standpoints. For example, Kostant-Rallis treated this subject from the Lie algebraic viewpoint, and considered the classical harmonic polynomials on $\mathbf{C}^p$ as polynomials on some specific vector space, which is canonically associated with the Lie algebra $\mathbf{so}(p, 1)$. In the series of papers we further investigate harmonic polynomials from their standpoint for the Lie algebras $\mathrm{su}(p, 1)$, $\mathrm{sp}(p, 1)$ and $\mathfrak{f}_{4(-20)}$. In particular in the previous paper we considered harmonic olynomials for the real rank 2 case $\mathrm{so}(p, 2)$, and obtained the formula of irreducible decomposition in the character level. In this paper we explain a method to decompose the space of harmonic polynomials into irreducible factors, and we explicitly give its decomposition for low degree cases.

Preface

We hope that these articles provide a comprehensive yet lively and up-to-date discussion of the state-of-the-art in information society, social systems, and the relevant research fields. We believe that this book contains a coherent view of the important unifying ideas throughout the many faces of systems approach and a guide to the most significant current areas of approach. We also appreciate that this book should contribute to build the ubiquitous society in Japan. We would like to thank Hiroshima Shudo University and the Faculty of Economic Sciences for financial supports of publishing this monograph. Also we would like to take the opportunity to thank Kyushu University Press for publishing this book and for authors for their contributions.

November, 2015
Munenori Kitahara
Hiroaki Teramoto

Contents

Preface i

Chapter 1 Audit and Compliance through Proactive Engineering Method
.... *Munenori Kitahara* 1
1. Introduction 2
2. The Clowd 24/7 4
3. Guarantee of Legality through Technology 6
4. Audit and Compliance 7
5. Information Systems and Regulations 10
6. Compliance through Information Technology 11
7. Architecture and Security Standard of Information Technology 14
8. Conclision 15

Chapter 2 Some Notes on Macroeconomic Policies:
  Abenomics in Japan .... *Chris Czerkawski and Osamu Kurihara* 19
1. Introduction 19
2. Three Arrows of Abenomics 21
3. Abenomics and the Empirical Responses 23
4. Why Abenomics May Not Be a Proper Policy for Japanese Economic Problems ? 26

Chapter 3 Health and Consumer Behavior .... *Hiroaki Teramoto* 35
1. Introduction 35
2. Analysis of Cost-effectiveness in Medical Care 36
3. Pollution and Health Production 41
4. Conclusion 44

Chapter 4 Measuring Global Flow of Funds:
  Theoretical Framework, Data Sources and Approaches .... *Nan Zhang* 47
1. Introduction 47
2. An Integrated Framework for Global Flow of Funds 48
3. The Data Sources for Global Flow of Funds 49
4. Global Flow of Funds Matrix on a From-Whom-to-Whom Basis 51
5. An Example for Setting up a Global Flow of Funds Matrix 54
6. Concluding Remarks 56

Chapter 5 A Comparative Study on Detecting Ridge Structure for Population-Based Optimization Algorithms ....*Setsuko Sakai and Tetsuyuki Takahama* 61
  1. Introduction 61
  2. Related Works 62
  3. Detecting Ridge Structure 63
  4. Differential Evolution with Detecting Ridge Structure 65
  5. Numerical Experiments 68
  6. Conclusion 76

Chapter 6 Explicit Irreducible Decomposition of Harmonic Polynomials in the Case of $\mathfrak{so}(p, 2)$ ....*Ryoko wada and Yoshio Agaoka* 83
  1. Introduction 83
  2. Preliminaries 84
  3. Irreducible Decomposition of S_n 85
  4. An Algorithm to Obtain the Explicit Irreducible Decomposition 91
  5. Tables of Generators of S_n and $\mathcal{H}_n$ for $n \leq 5$ 99
  6. Reproducing Formulas of the Principal Part of Irreducible Subspaces of $\mathcal{H}_n$ for $n \leq 5$ 103

Contributors 111

Chapter 1

Audit and Compliance through Proactive Engineering Method

Munenori Kitahara
Faculty of Economic Sciences, Hiroshima Shudo University
1-1 Ozuka-Higashi 1-chome, Asaminami-ku, Hiroshima, JAPAN 731-3195

Abstract

Legal states would require the residents and the entities of both lawful individual behaviors and business activities. The residents could receive online administrative, financial, commercial and educational services from the Web 24/7 on the Internet or the Cloud. It goes without saying that the entities have been developed the enterprises on the based upon the hi-powered information processing systems on the Internet or the Cloud.

Therefore, the systems should guarantee both the legality of behaviors and the compliance of enterprises. That is a problem of system architecture. That is, the systems have to be equipped with an architecture which can guarantee the legality and the compliance.

The architecture can be defined based on the ideas of "privacy by design," "security by default," and "IAM (identity and access management)." The concept is that the various requirements of laws, regulations and policies could be reached by an engineering method. That is, the systems would be designed upon those requirements. In other words, the requirements would be embedded into the architecture of systems.

To protect system, application, and information from internal and external threats and to comply with various regulatory, privacy and data protection requirements, organizations implement industry standard frameworks. IAM is as much an aspect of architecture as it is a collection of information technology components processes, and standard practices. As much as cloud IAM architecture and practices impact the efficiency of internal IT processes, they also play a major role in managing compliance within the enterprise.

There are left some unsolved problems. The one is a relationship between law and information technology. In fact, information technologies would control human's behaviors in spite of human's intention. The other is that whether it is right or not, that legal justice would be maintained by information technologies.

Key Words:

Audit, Compliance, Law and Computer, Fusion, ICT, Cloud computing, Security

1. Introduction

In these days, the residents could receive online administrative, financial, commercial and educational services from the Web 24/7 on the Internet or the Cloud. To advance information collaboration at the local government level, Government is promoting the wide spread adoption of regional information platforms—e-local governments. It goes without saying that the entities have been developed the enterprises on the based upon the hi-powered information processing systems on the Internet or the Cloud.

Corresponding to the informational environment, so-called information society law has been established. The law would rule people's information life. In the system of information society law, the laws have often introduced information technologies into the letter of the laws themselves. That is, the information technologies are defined as legal concepts in the laws. Therefore, performing the law would mean using the information technologies defined in the law.

These relationships can be called a collaboration of law and information technology. Through the collaboration, the laws can realize the own purposes with the aid of information technology. The customers can purchase goods via an internet shopping. Hotels also can perform an online room reservation. Therefore, the individual behaviors as well as the enterprise activities could be assumed not unlawful but lawful ones. The residents can pay tax by using an e-Tax system.

Those systems might guarantee legality of individuals' behaviors as well as compliance of organizations. The users only select messages and click icons on the browser. They would obey the law, if the messages and icons present the requirements of the law.

Audit functions take on increased importance in the cloud computing. Cloud service providers (CSPs) will face a large number of requests from the customers to prove that the CSP is secure and reliable. There a number of audit and compliance considerations for both the CSP and the customer to consider in cloud computing. Most IT service providers are adopting a combination of IT security frameworks and industry standards. Auditors should audit the requirements of the frameworks and standards. In addition, auditors must examine whether the systems fulfill the requirements because the requirements of laws were embedded into the systems. The auditors examine that the system will guarantee legality and compliance. Therefore, the auditors will be informed about the knowledge of law and information technology.

For examples, the electronic customer contract act requires customers of using an electromagnetic method, an electronic information system, e-mail technology and information communication technology. The electronic signature act also introduces an electromagnetic method and encryption technology. The internet minors protection act requires the providers of installing the information blocking and filtering technologies into the devices, which they sell to the minors.

These laws will achieve the purpose of law through letting the parties use an electromagnetic method. The electromagnetic method means a method of using electronic information processing system or other types of information communication technology. The method would be premised on using computer, other terminal devices, network, the Internet, application software, and computer program. The consumers or customers only select the messages and click the icons on the visual browser of the computer in order to purchase goods and services. These computer operations would not make legal issues such as unlawful actions. The reason is why the major requirements of the law are embedded in the systems. That is, the law is programmed into the systems. Therefore, the method will become to guarantee the legality of the computer operations. As the result, the law could maintain the effectiveness of the law itself. At the same time, it can be said that the law could realize the content of the law.

The consumers and customers used the information technologies in order to exercise their own legal rights from the viewpoint of the parties. They could exercise the legal rights and achieve the purpose of the contract with legality.

On the other hand, the information service provider (ISP) provides the IT infrastructure for the organizations and their users. The ISPs must provide the information systems installed with the architecture which will maintain the compliance with the related laws. The ISP should be responsible for implementing an architecture standard and security standard to protect systems, applications, and information and to comply with various regulatory, privacy and data protection requirements. To address those requirements, it might be recommended to deploy various information technologies.

The business entities could carry on the enterprises on the information systems complying with the related legal rules and various regulations. The information systems would have been designed on the rules, regulations and policies. Because the computers and the information systems would guarantee the compliance. In other words, the information technologies could lead the customers and the entities to lawful behaviors as well as complying enterprise activities.

Under the informational environment as mentioned above, it is necessary for both law and information technology to collaborate in order to achieve the purpose of the law while maintaining the legality and compliance. Moreover, one method should be adopted, how information technology can be imbedded into the letters of the law. The method might be called 'fusion of law and information technology.' The information technology will be given a legal authority through the fusion. As a result, information technology will become to be legally enforceable.

This method is the engineering one that has been adopted to practice privacy, data protection, and data security. The method is the same approach as privacy by design (PbD), and security by default (SbD). Therefore, the method might be called legality by design (LbD) and compliance by default (CbD). In these approaches, audit will increase the importance because the method is a proactive one.

This chapter has a couple of main purposes. First, this research will aim at presenting that a legal action will be guaranteed for legality and a system operating for compliance through a fusion of law and information technology. Thus, the author will show the outline of the cloud computing which has become widespread in the information ubiquitous society (Sec.2). He will elucidate the meaning that the information technology guarantees legality (Sec.3). The author will explain the audit for governance, compliance of IT organizations (Sec.4). There exist various regulations that IT organizations should comply with (Sec.5). Then, the author will propose that IT organizations should adopt a proactive engineering method, a fusion of law and information technology (Sec.6). Last, the author will propose that the law shall provide a security and architecture standard of the information technology (Sec.7).

2. The Cloud 24/7
2.1 Cloud and Ubiquitous Computing

The range of access devices for the cloud has expanded in recent years. Home PCs, enterprise PCs, network computers, mobile phone devices, custom handheld devices, and custom static devices (including refrigerators) are all online. Interestingly, the growth of the iPhone and the proliferation of applications available from its App Store illustrate an improvement in terms of access to the cloud. This greater access is resulting in greater use and growth of services within the cloud [1].

Users of multiple device types can now access applications and information from wherever they can load a browser. Indeed, browsers are becoming increasingly sophisticated. Enterprise applications can be accessed through a browser interface—a change from when a client (a so-called "fat") application needed to be loaded onto the desktop. The general population has become more familiar with the browser function and can use a discrete application, where the context is intuitive, without requiring training or user guides [2]. A suitable application programming interface (API) is another enabler for the cloud computing services delivery model. APIs empower users by enabling features such as self-provisioning and programmatic control of cloud services and resources.

Therefore, individual consumers today are already major users of cloud computing. They rely on cloud computing providers for many of their storage and computing requirements. Tax returns are now prepared through the cloud and stored in the cloud [3].

As a result, a tremendous amount of personal data resides in the cloud

2.2 Cloud Computing and Challenges

Cloud computing is steadily gaining acceptance within businesses, administrative and educational services. Although cloud computing is on its way to becoming a huge success and there are many benefits to cloud computing, there are reservations among cloud clients about using some cloud technologies [4].

Cloud computing, by virtualization, enables consumer to run instances of various operating system from having the same level of influence over the computing resources. Of great concern is the ability of consumers to assert quality of service. However, the law and standards bodies are a bit behind the times when it comes to virtualization. Many laws and standards assume that any given server is a physically distinct entity. Before moving into the cloud, the users must understand all of the relevant laws and standards which the applications and infrastructure are bound [5].

Although there are many benefits to adopting cloud computing, there are also some significant barriers to adoption. Two of the most significant barriers to adoption are security and privacy [6]. Security is a great concern for all the cloud clients when moving their data to the cloud. Although security in the cloud is generally reliable and proficient, cloud users need to know that the cloud provider they chose work with has a fully secure cloud environment. Because cloud computing represents a new computing model, there is a great deal of uncertainty about how security at all levels—network, host, application, and data levels—can be achieved.

The ability of cloud computing to adequately address privacy requirements has been called into question. Organizations face numerous different requirements attempting to protect the privacy of individuals' information, and it is not clear whether the cloud computing model provides adequate protection of such information, or whether organizations will be found in violation of requirements because of this new model. Cloud computing poses privacy concerns because the service providers may access the data that is on the cloud that could accidentally or deliberately be changed or even removed posing serious business trust and legal consequences [7].

The next challenge is that without knowing where all the cloud provider's assets reside. It is difficult to know with which legislation the consumer needs to comply. Furthermore, if the cloud provider has multiple centers worldwide, in many instances it is impossible to tell where in the world a particular consumer data set might be at any one point in time [8]. As for privacy and data protection, different countries and regions have different requirements regarding how personal information should be handled. In addition to the two, the notion "trust" is also very important for the cloud users [9].

Cloud service providers (CSPs) are obliged to challenge to establish, monitor, and demonstrate ongoing compliance with a set of controls that meets their customers' business and regulatory requirements, because there exist various challenges and barriers to cloud computing adoption in the enterprise, which are stated above. That is, CSPs must perform audit for compliance.

3. Guarantee of Legality through Technology
3.1 Observing Road Traffic Act

The road traffic act provides the maximum speed of cargo trucks on the highway. The enforcement ordinance of the road transport vehicle act also provides the maximum speed of 80 kilometers an hour on the highway. The drivers of the trucks had mostly not observed the legal speed. Then the road department of the Government revised the act and ordinance. The revised act required the large-sized cargo trucks of installing the speed suppression device with computer inside. The device can adjust the supply of fuel to track engine not to exceed the speed of 90 kilometers per hour, no matter how often the driver steppes on the gas pedal.

As for the maximum speed of the trucks, the drivers would seem to observe the road traffic act regardless of his intention. However, the intention of the law could be realized at that time. A speed suppression device with computer provided the drivers with a legality with road traffic act. That is, the tuck is apparently being driven within the legal speed according to the traffic act.

Cruise control systems also can keep cars in a legal speed. As the result, the drivers seemingly observe the traffic speed regulations. They worry about neither a patrol car nor a white police motorcycle.

In this case, there is a problem not to be resolved. The speed limiter will deprive the drivers of the right of emergency evacuation. There might occur a more dangerous accident that the trucks could avoid with the speed of 120 kilometers an hour, although other cars could run with the speed more than 150 kilometers.

3.2 Observing Electronic Consumer Contracts Law

In the information society, consumers purchase goods and services from the Web 24/7. An e-mail technology has been introduced into the Electronic Consumer Contracts Act. The article 2 (definitions) defines the electronic consumer contracts as follows:

"In this Act, an 'electronic consumer contract' means a contract that is made between a consumer and a business entity by electromagnetic method through a visual browser of a computer in cases where the consumer manifests his/her intention to make an offer or to accept the offer by transmitting his/her intention through his/her computer in accordance with the procedures prepared on this visual browser by the business entity or its designee." (Sec.1)

"In this Act, 'electromagnetic method' means a method using electronic information processing system or other types of information communication technology." (Sec.3)

"In this Act, 'electronic acceptance notice' means an acceptance notice to the offer of a contract which is, among electromagnetic methods, given by means of transmission through a telecommunication line connecting a computer, etc. (meaning a computer, a facsimile device, a telex or a telephone, the same shall apply hereinafter) used by the party dispatching the acceptance notice to the offer of the contract with a computer, etc. used by the offer or of the said contract." (Sec.4)

3.3 An Electronic Tax System and Tax Law

By using a national tax paying system (e-Tax), the residents can pay a national tax from their own home. Thanks to the e-Tax, they could fulfill the duty of taxpaying as a nation. The residents only use an electromagnetic method. They input several numbers and click icons or messages through a visual browser of a computer. A taxpayer clicks a paying button after connecting a card reader with an electronic certificate on in the end.

All the requirements of the tax laws had been embedded into the e-Tax system. It can be said that the requirements are programmed in the system. Therefore, the computer operations might follow the requirements of the tax laws. The actions all were lawful behaviors

4. Audit and Compliance
4.1 Governance

Governance implies control and oversight over policies, procedures, and standards for application development, as well as the design, implementation, testing, and monitoring of deployed services [10]. Governance is the managerial obligation of governing risk and control (GRC) for cloud computing and the virtualization technologies that enable cloud computing [11]. CSPs are challenging to meet the requirements of a diverse client base. To build a sustainable model, it is essential that the CSP establish a strong foundation of controls that can be applied to all of its clients. In that regard, the CSP can use the concept of GRC (Governance, Risk, and Compliance) that has been adopted by a number of leading traditional outsourced service providers and CSPs [12].

Cloud computing is a model for enabling convenient, on-demand network access to a shared pool of configurable computing resources (e.g., networks, servers, storage, applications, and servers) that can be rapidly provisioned and released with minimal management effort or service provider interaction.

In a SaaS model, the customer does not purchase software, but rather rents it for use on a subscription or pay-per-use model. In a PaaS model, the vendor offers a development environment to application developers, who develop applications and offer services through the provider's platform. An IaaS model also provides the infrastructure to run the applications. This model is similar to utility computing, in which the basic idea is to offer computing services in the same way as utilities.

These computing models have changed the governance structure of IT organizations [13]. Traditionally, most IT organizations govern the five technology layers (App, Services, Server, Storage, Network). The vendors have control over all the five layers in the SaaS, the three layers (Server, Storage, Network) in the PaaS, and the three layers (Server, Storage, Network) in the IaaS. Therefore, the IT organization's level of control diminishes and the level of cloud service providers (CSPs) increases [14]. However, although control increases for the CSP, responsibility remains with IT organization. It is critical for IT organizations to develop strong monitoring frameworks over the SPI (SaaS, PaaS and IaaS) delivery model to ensure that their service levels and contracted obligations are met.

4.2 Responsibility of CSPs

The SaaS model dictates that the provider manages the entire suite of applications delivered to users. Therefore, SaaS providers are largely responsible for securing the applications and components they offer to customers. Customers are usually responsible for operational security functions, including user and access management as supported by the provider. In the PaaS model, CSPs also are responsible for securing the platform software stack that includes the runtime engine that runs the customer applications. The CSPs are responsible for giving the enterprise customers the information necessary to perform risk assessment and ongoing security management. Network and host security monitoring outside the PaaS platform is also for the responsibility of the PaaS cloud provider. However, customers have full responsibility for securing their applications deployed in the IaaS cloud [15].

CSPs should also be responsible for an identity and access management. Traditional network controls are no longer relevant in the cloud and should be superseded by data security and identity-based controls [16]. Managing access control and governance within identity and access management (IAM) to meet today's business needs in the cloud remains one of the major reasons for enterprise adoption cloud services. IAM support for business needs ranges from secure collaboration with global partners to secure access for global employees consuming sensitive information from any location and any device at any time. The most important success factor for an enterprise to effectively manage identities and access control in the cloud is the presence of a robust directory and federated identity management capability within the organization — for instance, architecture and systems, user and access life cycle management processes, and audit and compliance capabilities [17]. Organizations implement industry standard frameworks to comply with various regulatory, privacy, and data protection requirements. IAM process and practice can help organizations meet objectives in the area of access control, operational security, and legal requirements.

Then, audit will be concerned in assuring security, privacy, and compliance in the cloud computing environment.

4.3 Objectives of Audit

To protect systems, applications, and information from internal and external threats and to comply with various regulatory, privacy, and data protection requirements, organizations implement a framework derived from industry standard frameworks [18]. The audit is a process whether organizations will perfectly comply with those regulations and requirements.

Audit and compliance refers to the internal and external processes that an organization implements to [19]:

· Identify the requirements with which it must abide—whether those requirements are driven by business objectives, laws and regulations, customer contracts, internal corporate policies and standards, or other factors

· Put into practice policies, procedures processes, and systems to satisfy such requirements

· Monitor or check whether such policies, procedures, and processes are consistently followed

Audit and compliance refers to the internal and external processes that an organization implements to:

· Identify the requirements with which it must abide -- whether those requirements are driven by business objectives, laws and regulations, customer contracts, internal corporate policies and standards, or other factors

· Put into practice policies, procedures processes, and systems to satisfy such requirements

· Monitor or check whether such policies, procedures, and processes are consistently followed.

4.4 Architecture of Information Systems

Driven by its strategy and requirements, the CSP must now determine how to architect and structure its services to address customer requirements and support planned growth. As part of the design, for example, the CSP will need to determine which controls are implemented as part of the service by default and which controls (e.g., configuration settings, select platforms, or workflows) are defined and managed by the customer [20].

Then, CSPs should adopt the concept of GRC. The GRC concept recognizes that compliance is not a point-in-time activity, but rather is an ongoing process that requires a formal compliance program [21].

4.5 Regulations

CSPs face an increasingly complex array of external compliance requirements from their customers, whether those include industry standards, regulatory regimes, or customer-specific frameworks. Frequently, those requirements are based on or refer to industry standards. As a result, using industry standards can be an effective compliance approach for CSPs if they can navigate through the ever-increasing number of standards that exist or are under development.

Many IT standards have a specific area of focus, such as [22]:
・Overall control environment/company-level controls
・Information security
・IT service delivery/operations
・Systems development
・Financial reporting systems
・Specific technologies
・Best practices Guidance
・Certification/Audit Criteria/Requirements
・Regulatory/Industry Requirements
・Audit Framework

5. Information Systems and Regulations
5.1 Cloud Computing and Regulations

Many current laws are difficult to apply to cloud arrangements because they do not cater adequately for the distinctive characteristics of cloud computing. Hence, analyzing legal issues with cloud is not always straightforward. Cloud computing isn't so much a technology as it is the combination of many preexisting technologies. These technologies have matured at different rates and in different contexts, and were not designed as a coherent whole; however, they have come together to create a technical ecosystem for cloud computing [23].

5.2 Various Regulations

Cloud service providers (CSPs) should pay attention to the discussions about how best control the behaviors of providers and customers (users) of cloud services. Being a trustworthy organization is important because it is a market advantage. The community (customers, users, providers, and regulators) must consider existing regulation requirements, regulatory frameworks, best practices, and other legal and corporate obligations [24].

The concepts of regulation, framework, benchmark, and standards are not the same, but they are closely related. There are a number of benchmarks, which are prescriptive sources of IT security settings for specific devices or applications [25], such as:
- Center for Internet Security (CIS) benchmark guidance
- Defense Information Security Agency (DISA) －Checklists, Security Technical Information Guides (STIG)
- National Institute of Standards and Technology (NIST) －Federal Information Protection Standards (FIPS)
- National Security Agency (NSA) －Security Hardening Guidelines
- Vendors (various) －hardening/security best practices

Many security frameworks are enforced by industry or become the basis for law [26]. These include:
- PCI－Payment Card Industry－for businesses who process credit cards
- NERC－National Electric Reliability Council－for utilities
- ISO/IEC 27001:2005－Information Security Management Systems Requirements－a framework for general IT systems security
- COBIT－Control Objectives for Information and related Technology－an IT Security and practices framework

In the United States, there exist a number of security regulations for business and governments including the following [27]:
- Federal Information Security Management Act
- Sarbanes-Oxley Law
- health Information Privacy Accountability Act
- Graham/Leach/Bliley Act
- Privacy Laws

6. Compliance through Information Technology
6.1 The Methodology of Fusion

At the earlier stage, it was conceived for the laws to collaborate with information technology in order to realize the intention of law [28]. Or the law aimed at realizing the purpose of itself though the combination of law and information technology. In a collaboration or combination, the component elements work jointly on an activity in which the component elements are individually distinct.

As for the information society law, information technology has been defined in the letter of the law. In other words, the technologies are embedded into the articles of the law, not vice versa. The two component elements are inseparably fused together. It means that the law would promote the addressees to use some kind of the technologies.

That is, the law shall aim at realizing the content of the law itself through the addressees' using those technologies.

In the electronic consumer contracts law, an electronic consumer contract means a contract that is made between a consumer and a business entity by electromagnetic method through a visual browser of a computer in cases where the consumer manifests his/her intention to make an offer or to accept the offer by transmitting his/her intention through his/her computer in accordance with the procedures prepared on this visual browser by the business entity or its designee. In the law, an electromagnetic method means a method using electronic information processing system or other types of information communication technology. In the law, an electronic acceptance notice means an acceptance notice to the offer of a contract which is, among electromagnetic methods, given by means of transmission through a telecommunication line connecting a computer used by the party dispatching the acceptance notice to the offer of the contract with a computer used by the offer or the said contract [29].

In this way, the consumers have only to operate the computer connected with the Internet to conclude an electronic consumers contract to buy goods on the Web. They only did click some messages and icons on the visual browser of the device. In other words, the consumers use the information technologies to exercise their legal right. Moreover, their operations would comply with the contract law. As a result, the information processing system provided their operations with a legality.

6.2 The Concept of Fusion

The method of fusion is to embed information technology into the law. As a matter of fact, the information technologies must be defined in the articles of the law. Then, the information technologies will be given a legal meaning. That is, the information technologies will have a legal authority as the other legal concepts.

Under the informational environment which information technologies are embedded into the letter of law, man would operate a computer, or an information system, and use information technology instead of performing the law as information. The users operate the device according to the messages on a visual browser of a computer. The operating procedures are written in the program of the system.

An electronic consumers contract means a contract that is made between a consumer and a business entity by electromagnetic method. The electromagnetic method would include using electronic devices and applications (computer, visual browser, electromagnetic information processing system, information communication technology). Then, operating these devices would be considered as a legal action. That is, sending an e-mail may be transmitting an offer or acceptance as a legal action. Therefore, the information technologies would be required of a legal standard on the architecture and security [30].

6.3 Proactive Method of Fusion

Both privacy law and data protection law are essentially proactive legal measures. There might be no perfect recovery in both cases after violating privacy and abusing personal data. The article 20 of the EU Data Protection Directive (95/46/EC) says that the processing operations are examined prior to the start thereof [31]. Privacy impact assessment (PIA) adopts an idea of privacy by design (PbD). The PbD is a proactive engineering method, because privacy was embedded in the systems. Where projects have encountered difficulties as a result of privacy intrusion, weak security of personal information, organizations and professionals involved will hopefully learn lesson and be more conscious of benefits of building in privacy from the outset in future work [32].

In that sense, the method of this fusion also will adopt a proactive engineering approach. The information system shall guarantee legality and compliance when major requirements of regulations are embedded into the systems. That is, using such a system will lead to a lawful actions and complying enterprises.

6.4 The Objectives of Fusion

There will be three main objectives in the fusion of law and information technology. The first objective is to guarantee a legality of consumers', customers', or users' operating procedures. The consumers want to conclude a sales contract on the Web. They have only to press keys or click icons according to the messages on the browser in practice. But, they were certainly performing their legal rights according to the electronic consumers contracts law. The operating procedures will become consistent with the content of the law.

The second one is to guarantee a compliance of ISPs with various regulations. Under a fused IT infrastructure, or informational environment, the organizations could achieve the compliance with various requirements, which would be required the entities in providing and operating the systems.

For the compliance, the architecture of the information systems will be very important. The ISPs should take account of an architecture standard in design and building the systems, which the related laws require. The laws will require the entities of the architecture based on 'security by default,' 'privacy by design,' 'data protection by default,' and 'identity/access management by design.'

The third objective is to put the words 'like cures like' into practice on the Internet through the fusion of law and information technology. That is, 'information technology cures information technology.' A hacker attacks a network with the same information technology as a networking engineer uses to protect the network.

Therefore, an information technology could prevent unlawful actions on the Web. Because the information technology has a legal basis through the fusion.

7. Architecture and Security Standard of Information Technology

7.1 The Necessity of the Standards

Under the fused informational environment, the addressees of law have no adequate knowledge of information technologies. The addressees would use the technologies as a customer, consumer, or tax-payer. They do not normally have enough time to follow the progress and change of the information technologies as well as the applications. Most information technologies have been never passed through technology impact assessment. The most important thing is that it is considered as a legal action to use the information technologies and operate the devices. Therefore, law should promulgate an architecture and security standard of information technologies.

7.2 Security Standard

Under the fused informational environment, the requirements of the core IT infrastructure will be presented, which are related to the architecture, user, data, operation from the viewpoints of security, data protection, privacy, compliance, and audit.

With securing an organization's core IT infrastructure at the network, host, and application levels, the threats must be examined, and the security policy must be written and communicated within the entity.

The requirements are related to user management, authentication management, authorization management, access management, data management and provisioning, monitoring and auditing.

7.3 Architecture Standard

To protect system, applications, and information from internal and external threats and to comply with various regulatory, privacy and data protection requirements, organizations implement an "IT general and application-level controls" framework deprived from industry standard frameworks [33]. Identity and access management (IAM) processes and practices can help organizations meet objectives in the area of access control and operational security. IAM is as much an aspect of architecture as it is a collection of technology components, processes, and standard practices. As much as cloud IAM architecture and practices impact the efficiency of internal IT processes, they also play a major role in managing compliance within the enterprise. Properly implemented IAM practices and processes can help improve the effectiveness of the controls identified by compliance frameworks [34].

An IAM with multi-layers and multi-functions is proposed [35]. The IAM is collection of technology components, processes, and standard practices. Standard enterprise IAM architecture encompasses several layers of technology, services, and processes. At the core of the deployment architecture is a directory service that acts as a repository for the identity, credential, and user attributes of the organization's user pool. The directory interacts with IAM technology components such as authentication, user management, provisioning, and federation services that support the standard IAM practice and processes within the organization.

In the areas of privacy protection, data protection, and information security, the architecture of the information systems which collect, use and disclose personal information, must attain a certain level. The reason why I would refer to the architecture is that I would like to solve such problems through an engineering methodology in design. This methodology is a proactive measure. Those kinds of problems should be solved through a proactive method. Therefore, the ideas of privacy by design through a privacy impact assessment, or a data protection impact assessment would provide the systems with the appropriate architecture level. In the long run, information systems will have to adopt almost the information technologies as described in the previous section.

8. Conclusion

This research aims at researching the relationships of law and information technology. I could find various affinities between law and information technology in the research through overcoming the previous problems. Moreover, I could find a few of the same characteristics in the information technology as law has.

I would like to explain the reasons why information technologies should be embedded into the law. First, the important features of computer system and network have been adopted in many social systems. Second, the information and networking technologies have ethical and social aspects. Therefore, information technologies could be affiliated to legal norms. Networking technologies, especially, are being used to link the two parties into closer relations with each other. Third, information technologies can guarantee a legality of behaviors. The technologies can contribute for organizations to comply with the laws. The information society can reach to a legal justice.

Is there the legitimacy in that individuals use information technologies in order to exercise the legal rights? An email is only a method of transporting an offer and acceptance notice between the parties in an electronic consumer contract. The information technology would provide no legal reasoning on the contract at all. The way of thinking is to be valid to the other fusion cases.

In the fusion, the more difficult problem is the way how the legislators describe the usage of information technologies in the articles of law. The electronic signatures act might provide an appropriate model. The act will suggest an introduction of the information technology, first of all. Then, the regulations of the law will promulgate the security and architecture of the information technology.

The important features of computer systems are adopted in many social systems in the information society. I could show the idea in that many important features of the technology have been adopted in the real political and social systems. The information systems have been contributing to social systems solutions.

Information security technology includes authentication technology, data protection technology and information filtering technology. These technologies would require the users of an ethical consideration. These technologies might lead the users to an ethical deed. Therefore, I would define that these information technologies are ethical technologies.

Information technologies have been being used in many legal fields. The fact might be an evidence that the information technology has legitimacy from the legal view point. The TCP/IP might, especially, be a law that controls behaviors of the internet users'.

It will be permitted that these technologies are used to realize the contents of laws in place of the laws. That is, this is a fusion of law and information technology. The fusion will aim at realizing legal justice.

There might be certainly various problems about the fusion. First, technologies will regulate technologies. Second, the fusion will force the users to use specific computer systems with the information technologies implemented. Third, the fusion will have to cope with the evolution of technologies. Last, there will be left the problem of standardizing the technologies.

Information society, increasingly, depends on computer systems to behave acceptably in applications with extremely critical requirements, by which she means that the failure of systems to meet their requirements may result in serious consequences.

References

[1] Tim Mather/Subra Kumaraswamy/Shahed Latif, *Cloud Security and Privacy*, O'Reilly, 2009, pp.12ff.

[2] *Ibid.*, p.13.

[3] Cf., *ibid.*, p.28.

[4] Cf., O. Arasaratnam, Introduction to Cloud Computing, in: B. Halpert (ed.), *Auditing Cloud Computing: A Security and Privacy Guide*,Wiley, 2011, pp. 9ff.

[5] Cf., George Reese, *Cloud Application Architectures: Building Applications and Infrastructure in the Cloud*, O'Reilly, 2009, p.63.

[6] Cf., Tim Mather et al., *ibid.,* p.31.

[7] Cf., M. Sajid/Z. Raza, Cloud Computing: Issues and Challenges, International

Conference on Cloud, Big Data and Trust 2013, Nov 13-15, RGPV, pp.35-41.

[8] Cf., O. Arasaratnam, *ibid.*, p.11.

[9] Cf., Siani Pearson, Privacy Security and Trust in Cloud Computing, in: Siani Pearson/George Yee (eds.), *Privacy and Security for Cloud Computing*, Springer, 2013, pp. 3 ff.

[10] Wayne Jansen/Timothy Grance, *Guidelines on Security and Privacy in Public Cloud Computing*, NIST, 2011, p.13.

[11] Cf., Mike Whitman/Herb Mattord, Cloud-Based IT Governance, in: B. Halpert (ed.), *ibid.*, p44.

[12] Cf., Tim Mather/Subra Kumaraswamy/Shahed Latif, *ibid.*, p.170.

[13] Tim Mather/Subra Kumaraswamy/Shahed Latif, *ibid.*, p.30.

[14] *Ibid.*

[15] Cf., *ibid.*, p.58.

[16] Cf., *ibid.*, pp.248ff.

[17] Cf., *ibid.*, p.251.

[18] Cf., Tim Mather/Subra Kumaraswamy/Shahed Latif, *Cloud Security and Privacy*, O'Reilly, 2009, p.75.

[19] Cf., *ibid.*, pp.183ff.

[20] Cf., *ibid.*, p.169.

[21] Cf., *ibid.*, pp. 170ff.

[22] Cf., *ibid.*, p.184.

[23] Cf., *ibid.*, p.11.

[24] Cf., Jeremy Rissi/Sean Sherman, Global Regulation and Cloud Computing, in: Ben Halpert (ed.), *Auditing Cloud Computing: A Security and Privacy Guide,* Wiley, 2011, p.144.

[25] *Ibid.*, pp.144-145.

[26] *Ibid.*, p.145.

[27] *Ibid.*, pp.146-147.

[28] See, M. Kitahara, Information Society Law in Japan, *US-China Law Review* Vol.8, No.1, 2011, pp,21-40.

[29] Andrew Murray, *Information Technology Law: The Law and Society*, Oxford Univ. Press, 2010, p.327

[30] See, C.Reed/J.Angel(eds.), Computer Law, 6th ed., Oxford, 2007, pp.553-554.

[31] Cf., David Wright/Paul De Hert, Introduction to Privacy Impact Assessment, in: David Wright/ Paul De Hert (eds.), *Privacy Impact Assessment,* Springer 2012, p.8.

[32] Cf., Nigel Waters, Privacy Impact Assessment — Great Potential Not Often Realized, in: David Wright/ Paul De Hert (eds.), *ibid.*, p.151.

[33] See, A. D. Kshemkalyani/M. Singhal, *Distributed Computing: Principles,*

Algorithms, and Systems, Cambridge University Press, 2008, pp.1-3.
[34] Kent Reichert, Use of Information Technology by Law Enforcement, Dec. 2001, pp.1-4. (http://www.sas.upenn.edu/jerrylee/programs/fjc/paper_dec01.pdf)
[35] Cf., Tim Mather et al., *ibid.*, pp. 73ff.

Chapter 2

Some Notes on Macroeconomic Policies : Abenomics in Japan

Chris Czerkawski* and Osamu Kurihara**
*Faculty of Economic Sciences, Hiroshima Shudo University
1-1 Ozuka-Higashi 1-chome, Asaminami-ku, Hiroshima, Japan 731-3195
** Faculty of Information Design and Sociology, Hiroshima Kokusai Gakuin University
20-1 Nakano 6 –chome, Aki-ku, Hiroshima, Japan 739-0321

Abstract

This paper is on macroeconomic policies known as Abenomics implemented in Japanese economy under so-called three arrows policy. The paper summarizes the nature of Japanese economic crisis, the instruments implemented to foster economic growth and stimulate demand, the empirical consequences of the measures applied in the last ten years. The effectiveness of these measures is discussed in context of economic theories of crisis, the empirical results confirmed by statistics and in international comparative context. The failures and shortcomings of these policies are presented and conclusions drawn on existing potential for resolving the crisis.

Key words:

Abenomics, Macroeconomic policies, Japan's economic crisis

1. Introduction

The conventional answer to the question of Japanese economy crisis is to blame the so- called liquidity trap which was enhanced by unfavourable demographics which, in turn, slowed down demand for investment. It was also believed that fiscal spending/release investment plus negative interest rate may lead to the growth of inflationary expectations and hopefully higher GDP growth. This rationalization may be a conceptual background for the policies implemented in Japan under the name of Abenomics. This logic was very much in line with the monetary economics prescriptions introduced originally by economist Milton Friedman. He was calling for large scale asset purchases (LSAPs) long before it was widely practiced and understood that for the purchases to help the economy there must be a sufficiently large and *permanent* expansion of the monetary base. On the latter point, Friedman knew that even though the monetary base and treasuries may be almost perfect substitutes in a zero lower led environment, they may not be the same in the future. And since investors make decisions on what they think will happen in the future, a monetary base expansion that is expected to be continuing and greater than the demand for the it in the future is likely to affect current spending [1].

Yet, the economic theory behind quantitative easing (QE) has never been universally supported by empirical evidence. For this theory to apply, there must be a ongoing increase in the monetary base. Yet after the Bank of Japan's experiment with QE, the added reserves were all rapidly withdrawn in early 2006 and Prime Minister Shinzo Abe has committed the government to a radical reverse of monetary policies that was similar in spirit to FDR's actions in 1933. This program, called Abenomics, aimed to permanently double the size of the monetary base and end the deflation. It was extensively engaged in asset purchases that are triple the size of the Fed's relative to GDP. Hence, the Bank of Japan has committed to even larger asset expansion which again may be in line with Milton Friedman recommendations.

The theory behind QE is that if the CB replaces an interest bearing asset (bonds) with a non-interest bearing asset (cash), that the holders of that cash would find a way to make it generate interest. The main problem with this theory, and why it takes so much QE to lift prices, is that if someone was content on sitting on < 1% interest bearing bonds, already giving up opportunities to liquidate those bonds to loan or purchase other stock instead, it's because they just don't have better options. They elected to receive minimal interest for the privilege of storing extra profit almost risk-free.

The quantitative easing depends obviously very much on public expectations and Bank of Japan aims at 2% inflation by printing money until the inflation target is reached. One can easily observe that printing additional money will be inflationary and if the public expect inflation, they can bring it about by demanding higher wages, higher prices etc.

Consumers would expect that increases in money supply lead to some changes in prices levels and some changes in output levels (GDP). The Phillips curve more or less implies that the output changes will take place first, and the price level changes will take place, once output cannot change much further. If the individual investors do not believe the accuracy of governmental target of 2% they would not invest against the trends supported by Japanese central bank. If everyone invests accordingly to BOJ policy, then the policy would probably succeed.. Doubling the money supply *should* double the price level, *over time*. However, the question is, *how long will it take* for the price level to double? That depends on the slope of the short-run Phillips Curve, which by all accounts, is very flat in Japan. All this reasoning is correct however under the assumption of deflation being the root of the crisis.

There is however another answer which does not regard long-lasting deflation as a root cause of the problem. The answer may lie in structural excess of corporate earnings over investment. Available data suggest that in the past decade profitability in Japanese corporations grew steadily but new investment remained at low levels. Logical conclusion would be to transfer excess funds generated by the corporate sector via higher corporate taxes with the corresponding growth in dividends and wages which would result in enhanced demand. This may be economically justified policy yet, because of its strongly pro-business bias, may not be supported by the current government in Japan.

It is sometimes agreed that Japanese economy offers the best example of long-lasting deflation [2]. The period of deflationary pressures has been relatively easy, with a cumulative fall in consumer prices of just 4% between 1998 and 2012, but very persistent, lasting for more than a decade. This was followed by a decline in share and land prices beginning in the early 1990s, after strong growth in asset prices and credit in the second half of the 1980s. The following decline in asset prices worsened bank balance sheets and resulted in a so-called lost decade for growth between 1991 and 2000. Since growth has, in fact, never returned to rapid growth period, the entire post-1991 period is often referred to as "two lost decades". The statistics support this conclusion [3].

Although purchasing power parity (PPP) adjustments aren't always perfect, they are often used for comparisons precisely because of the frequent volatilities in currency markets. Looking at the PPP-adjusted figures Japan's economic decline is very well evidenced. In 1991, its real output per capita was 87% of that in the US; in 2011 that figure had fallen to 72%. For most of the 1990s, Japan was the second richest per capita large economy in the world. Then it became poorer than all of those economies except for Italy. In 1987, Japan's real output per person reached 98% of Germany's, and from 1988 to 1998 its income was higher than that in Europe's strongest economy. In 2011, its real GDP per capita stood only at 92% of that in Germany. Japan has underperformed and fallen behind Western Europe, USA, Canada even though these economies also experienced a moderate slow down in the same period.

The economic factors cannot, however, fully explain the economic decline of the last twenty years. Perhaps even more important are changing demographic factors. The fast ageing population and decline in active productive population had a major impact on the relationship between deflation and economic performance. On a per capita basis, real GDP growth slowed markedly during the 1990s, but actually *rose* during the 2000s. Between 1991 and 2000, cumulative per capita real GDP grew by a 6%, compared with 26% in the United States. Between 2000 and 2013, however, cumulative per capita real growth was only 10%, compared with roughly 12% in the United States. Real GDP per working age population, a measure that also takes into account the effect of ageing on economic performance, shows an even stronger performance. It indicates that cumulative growth in the period 2000-13 exceeded 20% in Japan, compared with roughly 11% in the United States). In the period 2000-07, cumulative per capita real GDP growth in Japan and the United States were, respectively, about 9% and 11% and, when growth is measured in terms of working age population, about 15% and 8%. [4].

In consequence of the deteriorating economic growth Japanese PM Shinzo Abe introduced a series of economic reforms promising to re-inflate the economy at any cost, mostly by extensive increase in public spending. This was later formalized in so-called three arrows of economic policies discussed later. A number of monetarist-leaning academics expressed hopes that "Abenomics" would revitalize the Japanese economy. This sentiment was expressed by monetarist-leaning economists such as Matt Yglesias, Joe Weisenthal, Scott Sumner and others. Even those who were less enthusiastic on the Abenomics believed that key element of this policy ie significant weakening of central bank independence and efforts to eliminate deflation would constitute an important experiment in monetary policy [5].

The purpose of this paper is thus to give a brief and critical evaluation of the Abenomics in view of economic theories of crisis, the empirical data discussed in comparative and international context.

2. Three Arrows of Abenomics

Abenomics has been formalized in official governmental documents as well as in a number of research papers [6]. Its purpose was to slow down or stop certain negative trends in Japanese economy and stimulate economic growth.

The main targets of governmental policies became: near zero growth for the past twenty years; decline in consumer spending, depressed consumer sentiments due to the 2011 earthquake disaster and negative consequences resulting in a recession in 2012, as well as government debt due to extensive spending from the 1990s.

The other targets included: long term deflation; and overvalued strong yen, damaging exports, low unemployment coupled with long-term concerns about labor availability as Japan's population is declining; growing shortages of labor force in some areas (eg. construction), low female labor participation rate and a large portion of the labor force non-permanent employment with lower incomes and benefits. These negative phenomena were to be fought with a series of dramatic policy instruments known as three arrows of Abenomics. They included:

2.1 1st Arrow: Monetary Expansion

Monetary Expansion or "Monetary Easing" is a monetary policy used by central bank by buying formal assets from commercial banks thus rising the prices of those assets and lowering their yield while increasing the monetary base. Bank of Japan accomplished this by buying more governmental bonds than would be required to set interest rate to zero. Also asset-based securities and equities were purchased with the resulting commercial bank current account raised from Yen 5 trillion to Yen 35 trillion in the period of 2001-2005.

The intention was that the increasing price levels by creating more money may break the deflationary cycle and induce consumers to stop saving and start spending.

2.2 2nd Arrow: Expansive Fiscal Policy

The main characteristic feature of this policy was to spend more in order to boost the Japanese economy. Statistics from the Japanese government show that government spending has been significantly increasing over this period.

The most extensive spending were in three areas 1) welfare; 2) servicing the debt: 3) public works. The welfare targeted spending is explained by Japan's rapidly aging population, the second because Japan's debt is already highest among developed countries , and the third is largely linked with infrastructure investment, particularly in relation to the Tokyo 2020 Olympics.

Increased spending had to be balanced with more active tax policies. The most visible element here was the consumption tax increase to 8 % with the further increase to 10% at the later stage. Here, while trying to increase growth through government spending, the Japanese government is trying to rebuild their finances, or at least reduce their reliance on debt.

2.3 3rd Arrow: Pro-Investment Structural Reforms

This is a combination of various policies intended to stimulate economic growth and productivity in longer period. It includes several areas of socio-economic activity.

1) Lowering corporation tax. In the first stage Corporation Tax has been lowered in by 2.4%. with possibility of further lowering.
2) Increasing the labor participation of women due to Japan's population and labor force is declining and Japan's female labor participation rate being   is one of the lowest among the developed world. Bringing women into the work force is a way to release additional workforce into the economy. In addition government will aim at providing for more childcare workers and childcare facilities.
3) Opening economy to foreign skilled workforce includes fast-tracked permanent residency for "highly-skilled" foreigners and bringing more foreigners into Japanese universities through the G30 program. Also additional funds to send more Japanese students overseas with scholarships in particular in technology, high-tech and informatics.
4) "Cool" Japan which aimed at stimulation of Japanese exports of foods and other products to the world and support for such corporations. Also, measures to increase inbound tourism and lowering of visa restrictions and introduction of duty-free shopping.
5) Further easing of trade barriers and regulations, promotion of free trade, participation in the Trans-Pacific Partnership with   lowering of barriers to foreign direct investment in Japan. Deregulation in many industries such as healthcare, agriculture, transportation and services.

Some of these have been implemented already and some are still in the process of administrative planning. The main difference between the first two arrows and the third one is that the aim of the former ones was to stimulate growth in the short period while the latter one aims to secure Japan's long term growth and economic health, and therefore needs time to take effect [7]

3. Abenomics and the Empirical Responses

The "three arrows":   monetary easing to reverse deflation, fiscal stimulus to boost immediate spending, and structural reforms to revive long-term growth have been gradually introduced by the government. The evaluation of the effectiveness of these policies varies widely according to the economists and practitioners. The "court economists" around PM Abe are very supportive of the policies while there is a large group of professional experts who are highly critical. In between there is a growing number of economists who are at least increasingly critical about the mechanism of reform and its empirical results [8].

According to the governmental economists all three arrows reached their targets and the economy is in a process of slow yet gradual recovery. Yet two of the instruments have already been used and any stimulus from temporary spending has been more than offset by premature tax hikes made to cut government debt. Meanwhile, the prospects for structural reform have not really progressed.

That leaves just one real arrow: monetary easing. But none of the three arrows can work without the other two. Confidence must rest on something more substantive than inflation: meaningful structural reforms to reverse Japanese companies' lagging competitiveness. Otherwise, any temporary economic expansion may be mjch less effective than originally desired [9].

The major macroeconomic aim of Abenomics - ie moving economy from deflationary to inflationary stage of growth by encouraging growth of prices has not been satisfactorily achieved. Most of that price rises in the last two years resulted from a 25 percent decline in the value of the Japanese yen, which raised prices on imports as well as on products made from those imports. It may also be argued that depreciation of the yen effectively transfered income from Japanese consumers and firms to foreign oil suppliers, food producers and manufacturers. Besides, since the yen has more or less stabilized, the inflationary effect of the depreciation is likely to wither.

In period of 1997-2012, wages in Japan have fallen by nine percent in real terms. They are expected to continue falling, despite highly advertised wage hikes by a some companies whose profits from overseas sales have been artificially boosted by the weaker yen. The government claim that wages will rise once workers and firms come to expect inflation. This may be an example of wishful thinking as there is another view supported by some evidence according to which deflation is not the cause of Japan's problems but a symptom of another structural imbalance between corporate incomes and investment.

The other aim of Abenomics – depreciation of the yen – some 25 percent to the US dollar did not prove to be particularly beneficial. Depreciation can cheapen the price of exports in overseas markets, helping a country export more. But the other side of the argument is that imports become more costly, and in Japan's case, the harm suffered by consumers and companies has probably severely outweighed the benefits enjoyed by exporters. The real volume of exports has slightly risen since the start of Abe's term but the countrys problem is not that the yen is overvalued but that the companies are no longer creating the innovative products that are competitive in world markets. Car exports do not rise because Toyota Motors and Nissan continue to shift production offshore rather than exporting from Japan. The fact that Japan ran a trade deficit despite a currency exchange rate that, in price-adjusted terms, is the cheapest since the 1970s, suggests that Japanese companies experienced a dramatic fall in international competitive power. [10].

The second arrow, fiscal stimulus, was supposed to give consumers the money they needed to spend more. This could be achieved by tax cuts or the properly targeted spending. In retrospect it seems, however, that the government expanded public spending has resulted in even bigger slow down in consumer spending. The new spending measures, have been more than offset by his raising of the consumption tax from five percent to eight percent. Another hike, to ten percent, was scheduled for October 2015 but how can people spend more when Abe leaves them with less money to spend?

Japan's post war economic history of trade surpluses made the country a huge net lender. Even if it runs a small trade deficit, its massive foreign exchange reserves were large enough to prevent capital from fleeing. This may be an example of an interesting contradiction of Japanese monetary policy. While on one hand, Japan finances its own government debt, the Bank of Japan has proved its ability to keep interest rates down. On the other hand, BOJ seems to ignore this fact when it supports interest rate hike without any belt-tightening measures.

Many economists, mentioned above, believe that Abe's tax hike will depress economic growth for some time. And if there is a further spending cut to respond to Ministry of Finance goal of reducing budget deficit by 50% the growth prospects may be reduced for much longer time. This may be a premature move and perhaps Japan should first restore growth and then work on the deficit.

The third arrow – structural reform – will probably determine whether Japan can raise its long-term real growth rate from the 0.8 percent average prevailing since 1992 to the two percent the government planned. Even Japanese government economists admit that without reform, the country's long-term growth rate will never exceed around 0.5 to 1.0 percent. With the working-age population shrinking, the only way to generate more growth is to gain more productivity from each worker. The indicators of Japan's GDP per hour show that this country is, on average, behind other industrialized economies by roughly 25 %. Yet the erosion of human capital caused by the rise of irregular workers makes raising productivity even more difficult [11].

The process of restructuring of Japanese economy will necessarily replacing old, inefficient and outdated firms with the ones based to high-tech technologies. The sectors of Japan's economy that face international competition, such as the auto industry, enjoy high productivity. But the gross share of the economy is still domestically oriented, and much of it is protected from both international and domestic competition by domestic regulations and cartel-like business practices. In these sectors, Japan still lags far behind its competitors. One particular example is consumer services sector with its overstaffed, overregulated and time-consuming structures.

On the other hand, if reform aimed at rising labour efficiency were easy, it would have been accomplished long ago. The problem is that reforms aimed at promoting competition would hurt many entrenched firms and their workers. Since a Japanese worker's current job at his current firm is his main social safety net, a desire to avoid social dislocation is the main reason Japan protects non-competitive companies. Therefore common and easily observed cases of inefficient business practices will probably slow down potential for growth particularly in service and agricultural sectors in future.

In the past, Japan has introduced reforms that worked, such as deregulating the financial market, forcing resistant banks to clean up the massive nonperforming loans that were slowing down economic growth, ending laws that allowed small stores to block the entry of larger ones into their neighborhoods, and giving new entrants in the cell-phone business equal access to the mobile infrastructure of a previously dominant monopoly. These reforms resulted in productivity gains in retail and telecommunications sectors, and in many instances opened distribution channels for newcomers.

The third arrow of Abenomics is a very watered down version of the past reforms. The proposed agricultural reform, for example, would merely replace a subsidy focused on production levels with one focused on income, while giving no real incentives for tiny inefficient farms to consolidate or for agribusiness to expand sufficiently. Proposals to increase career opportunities for women misses the main problem that most of females get taken off the promotion track once they become pregnant. Furthermore while Abe has raised taxes on consumers VAT, he strongly promotes cutting taxes on corporations. The belief that this would promote investment is incorrect, as. Japan's corporations already have far more cash than they choose to invest in Japan In fact, corporate tax cut might raise stock prices and gain Abe more corporate support.

The other test of the third arrow is Abe's handling of the negotiations for the Trans-Pacific Partnership. The progress in this area was slow because government insisted on keeping tariffs and other barriers high in a few agricultural sectors (such as beef, dairy, and pork) that employ less than 100,000 households but where high prices boost Japan Agriculture's income. Even if a accession treaty is eventually signed, Abe's support for special interest groups that support his party means that it won't be used as a catalyst for domestic reform. unlike the way South Korea used its trade agreements with the United States and Europe.

4. Why Abenomics May Not Be a Proper Policy for Japanese Economic Problems?

There is a rising skepticism regarding the general assumptions of Abenomics. Here, the core criticism is focused on macroeconomic foundations of these policies especially that the policy is too much focused on the demand side of its economy, not on the supply side and the policy is ignoring the most dramatic socio-economic problem – demographics.

With the growing gap between people in productive age and the non-productive group (below 18 and over 60 years old), the potential for growth declined. This brings about a number of problems for the Japanese economy. Firstly, the government commitment in spending on pensions, medical expenses and social security will continually act as a substantial burden to the already indebted country with a public debt of 240% its GDP. This will further worsen the financial integrity of the Japanese government leading to a further erosion of international confidence in Japanese economy. The lack of confidence can raise the risk premium for new investment projects . Secondly, its declining workforce cannot sustain the economic output level that has been maintained in the past. The Japanese demography will drastically deteriorate even more so that more young people will have to support for the older population, which in turn may imply that this change in demography is the main culprit for the last two decades of deflation and stagnant economic growth.

So the fundamental demography problems were not really addressed and , the government still believes that problem is of lack of demand. The problem is that households won't spend today because they think goods will get cheaper tomorrow. In effect, even if they hold cash at the bank earning zero interest, deflation means that they are getting a comfortable *real return*. The policy goal of Abe government to make that real return negative for average Japanese. And the only way to create a negative real return when interest rates are zero is to have inflation. If government can persuade the consumers that inflation is on the rise in the future, then they will, hopefully, cut savings and increase consumption now – or so the theory goes.

The logic of governmental economists, which dominated Abenomics, was that if the economy is working below potential with unused capital and labour, any sudden jump in demand may result in higher wages and greater government tax receipts. Consequently, the raised spending will result in higher wages and living standards in the future. This was conventional, Harvard Business School prescription for a classic win-win situation – more consumption and more growth. This however poses a number of problems which potentially may destabilize the whole policy. In particular how smoothly this all works depends to a large extent on size of the output gap.

At the end of 2015 there were more signs from the market which indicated that Abenomics may not be working according to expectations. Statistics confirm that companies cut earnings forecasts because of poor consumer spending, a key growth indicator for Japan at a time when exports and factory output are low. "Consumer spending has ground to a halt," according to Noritoshi Murata, president of Seven & i Holdings. "There are a lot of concerns about the global economy and not many positives for consumption. Weak spending could continue into the second half of the fiscal year." Real wages, adjusted for inflation, rose 0.5% in July 2015 compared with the previous year. That was the first gain in 27 months. But wage growth subsequently slowed to 0.2% in August, and summer bonuses fell from last year, government data shows. Another problem is that more workers are forced to accept jobs with low pay. Part-time and irregular workers comprised a record 37.4% of the workforce last year, according to the National Tax Bureau. Irregular workers earn on average less than half of what regular full-time workers earn according to the data from Ministry of Finance (see Alternative Economics, 12 October 2015).

An alternative to Abenomics is unviable both on logical as well as practical grounds. First, one cannot argue for an alternative to the whole strategy which was based on ideological grounds firmly based on a mix of intensive governmental interventionism and preferences for big corporations. According to this view, an expansionist fiscal policies benefiting largest corporations would yield higher investment, output and bring about higher economic growth. This did not materialize and there is a danger that Japan may again fall into what economists call a quintuple dip recession.

Second, there is no real alternative to these policies from the opposition parties in Japan. It seems that no real political power would risk a policy which would be in conflict with long-term business prospects of big corporations. The long-lasting business, personal, systematic and structural bonds between politicians and big business in Japan make any real alternative to Abenomics unthinkable. And conservative passivism of Japanese voters makes it second to impossible to elect government which would propose more radical changes. Therefore, there is no real chance to modify Abenomics to force a redistribution of incomes in Japan. On the other hand, there is little chance to move to more free economy with less governmental interventionism.

In this paper the alternative view is suggested ie that Japan's growth decline is principally a supply-side issue – the direct result of an ageing workforce and slower productivity gains from technology. If, therefore, Japan's output gap is relatively small, expansive monetary and fiscal policies may not work. If conditions change, it may end up with the Bank of Japan owning the Japanese government bond market if conditions change. And this will be at the very time when central government revenues are collapsing coupled with the asset bubble and bonds issues rise to cover growing budget deficits. Should there be a panic in financial markets in Japan – those who can get rid of yen-denominated risk assets will have only one place to go: abroad. The yen, therefore, will take another sharp movement down, leading to further cost-push inflation (and perhaps capital controls). Of course, this monetary experiment will end up with a lower standard of living for the Japanese people through the collapse in the yen and general financial market instability[12].

This is just one of examples of unfortunate yet still possible scenarios which are not designed in Japan but are result of changes in international economic cycles and caused by transfer of international financial shocks into Japan. One of the most visible byproducts of rising international competitive problems may have been almost 20 years of Japan's deflationary period. In such a framework the government have carried out, largely ineffective, extraordinary macroeconomic policies which have resulted in huge amounts of public debt and BOJ liabilities, in the form of reserve deposits, to future generations.

Japan's economy has no other choice but to adapt to the ongoing shift in changing growth conditions and the more competitive international environment. Capital investment expanded as exports grew during Japan's longest postwar period of economic expansion. But net investment - the amount spent on capital assets, less depreciation – did not follow this trend. Net capital expenditures are intended to foster consumption in economy. The current downward trend in capital investment on a net basis suggests that companies anticipate consumption will prefer to stabilize at the current level. This reflects the economy's long-term shift toward maturity, and cannot be easily changed by applying policy tools such as lower corporate tax rates.

Perhaps it may be time for the government to give up economic growth and inflation as policy objectives. In light of long term trends in the Japanese economy, the nation could switch the principal aim of its reform efforts away from real GDP growth. Instead, measures such as labor market reform and improvement of demographics should aim to create an environment in which the high levels of production seen today in Japan can be sustained. The priority may be given instead to the sustainability of its public finances.

Perhaps government should realize that inflation, when considered outside of the context of Japan's economy as a whole, is meaningless. Declines in crude-oil prices and favorable supply factors could be expected to push inflation considerably down. It may be that they will moderately but steadily improve trade terms and Japan's economic health. Japan may not need drastic measures that throw the economy into high-risk situation; rather it needs carefully thought out stable and balanced policies that can keep more or less resistant to external crises and preserve relatively high standards of living[13].

This view may be supported by a growing number of economic analyses showing that the Abenomics policies were based on many uncertain and unverifiable assumptions both of theoretical as well as empirical nature. The most important include:

1. There is a good reason to believe that currency depreciation may not work in line with the "beggar thy neighbor" policy as there is nothing to stop competing nations to use the same instrument against country depreciating its currency. Moreover the mechanic effect of depreciation weakens in time and is countered by the income effect of depreciation which works in opposite direction [14].

2. There is an ongoing discussion whether inflationary expectations play such a big role in economic expansion. In other words was deflation a root problem of Japanese economic slow down?. The follow up questions seem logical – are governmental macropolicies capable of 'forcing' consumers to buy more? Will the rapidly aging population be inclined to spend more on more expansive goods and services? Will the consumer tax rise stimulate demand? The answer to all these problems is most probably NO. The measures introduced by Abe government may in fact be in conflict with higher demand target.

3. There are serious doubts about the effectiveness of fiscal spending vis-à-vis economic growth. First the value of fiscal/Keynesian multiplier which forms the logical ground for expansive fiscal policies is very uncertain according to various estimates. According to some it is 0.5 according to others 0.9; 1.4 or 1.7[15].

Many studies show that fiscal deficit leads to recession not to recovery and according to the well known study by Rogoff/Rainhart 85-90% debt to GDP ratio would require some 5-7 years to restore growth rate in economy. There seems to be a correlation between high budget deficit and recession but what is the cause and what is result – opinions differ[16].

There is rather uncertain empirical evidence for Abenomics in this respect. Ion 1998-2007 Japan's average budget deficit was 6.7% of GDP with real growth rate of 1%. In the same time USA had 2% budget deficit with 3% growth and the Euro group of countries 1.9% budget deficit with real growth rate 2.3%. Here the evidence points to a negative correlation between high budget deficits and economic growth[17].

According to some estimates with the frictional unemployment rate at around 3.5% and the current unemployment rate at 4.2%, there are actually not much idle reserves in the economy. Based on some growth forecast, the year-end jobless rate is set to reach 3.7% in 2013, 3.6% in 2014 and 3.4% in 2015. Because of strong deflationary expectations, there will probably be only limited rise in inflation initially, despite a narrowing output gap. One can expect inflation to start to pick up once the economy reaches full employment in late 2015. Consequently, the year-end inflation forecasts (excluding impact of consumption-tax hikes) were much lower than expected ie 0.4% in 2013, 0.8% in 2014 and 1.6% in 2015 [18].

In the short and medium term upward pressure on long-term rates should also intensify alongside accelerating inflation. However, the BoJ would probably not be able to tighten policy, because it would be concerned about the possibility of causing a bond-market crisis that could lead to financial instability (given that the most of Japanese government bonds are held by domestic financial institutions). When the central bank becomes deeply incorporated into the government's debt management, price stability may be sacrificed in order to achieve financial-system stability. But the BoJ won't be able to neutralise this upward pressure for long, and the long-term interest rate may also rise in the latter part of 2015 or early 2016, increasing the risk of a fiscal crisis.

The third arrow of Abenomics should put more emphasis on promotion of innovation by enforcing laws against anticompetitive practices, labor flexibility (rather than the use of irregular workers), and financing a solid safety net. Instead, the present government, has moved in the opposite direction, promoting mergers among troubled firms. Countries such as Sweden spend up to 1.5 percent of GDP on programs for ongoing adult education, job matching, and the like to help workers shift from job to job, but Abe's fiscal austerity rules out similar steps. This "saving" is not at all economical and will result in higher socio-economic costs in labour restructuring in future.

There is also a problem of Japanese population getting older and still unresolved problem of expanding market for services and goods for senior population. This coupled with rapidly changing gender balances – with females outliving males by 8 years, and the declining of population involved in creating GDP will necessarily worsen the growth prospects for the economy and the successful implementation of Abenomics.

There is a growing concern both among economist and general public that Abenomics is not a proper medicine for Japanese socio-economic crisis. So far, it rather helped gain popular support to carry out with other political agenda – security and history issues. This however may be much short-lived assumption and the economic mismanagement may become evident much sooner than expected. According to some surveys eighty percent of Japanese polled say that his policies have failed to improve their lives at all. Abe remains popular probably because there is no real alternative in Japan political system and the main parties engaged in futile internal infighting, without any visible trace of consistant or coherent socio-economic vision for future. Sooner or later, however, its failures will become impossible to ignore, and Abe may lose the political will and power to make necessary reforms[19].

References

[1] The importance of the public believing the monetary base expansion will be permanent can be illustrated by looking back to the early part of the Great Depression. At that time the monetary base grew rapidly between 1929 and early 1933 compared to previous growth. Yet during this time the money supply and nominal GDP continued to fall. The reason this monetary base growth did not slow down the collapse of financial intermediation and aggregate spending is because it was still tied to the gold standard. Consequently, the public did not expect a large, permanent expansion of the monetary base. But that all changed with FDR in 1933. He created so called "monetary regime shift" both by signaling a desire for a higher price level and by abandoning the gold standard which led to even more rapid monetary base expansion. FDR's actions caused the public to expect a permanent monetary base expansion that would raise future nominal income and a sharp recovery followed in 1933.

[2] See for example, Krugman, Paul. "The Return of Depression Economics and the Crisis of 2008", W.W. Norton Company Limited, [2009]; Ohno, K., "Economic Development of Japan", National Graduate Institute for Policy Studies. [3 April 2011]; Sumner, S. "Why Japan's QE didn't "work". The Money Illusion. [November 24, 2014]; Amyx, J., Japan's Financial Crisis: Institutional Rigidity and Reluctant Change. Princeton University Press. pp. 17–18 [2004]; Leika K., "Japan eyes end to decades long deflation". Reuters. [September 7, 2012]; Fletcher III, W. Miles, and Peter W. von Staden, eds., Japan's 'Lost Decade': Causes, Legacies and Issues of Transformative Change Routledge, [2014]; Funabashi, Y., and Barak Kushner, eds. Examining Japan's Lost Decades, Routledge, [2015]; Hayashi, F., and Edward C. Prescott. "The 1990s in Japan: A lost decade." Review of Economic Dynamics [2002] pp: 206-235. [2002]; Tabuchi, H., "When Consumers Cut Back: An Object Lesson From Japan". The New York Times, 22 09 2009.; Krugman, Paul "The Return of Depression Economics and the Crisis of 2008" [2009] W.W. Norton Company Limited See also, BIS Quarterly Review, March 2015. For more comprehensive sources on Japanese economy see Bank of Japan and Ministry of Finance official statistics.

[3] In 2007, Japan's nominal output per capita was 74% of the USA. Only when the dollar fell 38% against the yen, and only then nominal Japanese output per capita became 96% of the USA. It took almost two decades to recover from the income decline and only in 2010 did its economy regain a level of income last attained in 1995.

[4] On the role of demographic factors in Japanese growth see, "Japan population to shrink by one-third by 2060". BBC News. January 30, 2012; "Japan's Population Falls by Record in 2012 as Births Decrease". Bloomberg.; Hashimoto, R., (attributed). General Principles Concerning Measures for the Aging

Society. Ministry of Foreign Affairs of Japan. [05 03 2011]; McCurry, J., "Japan's age-old problem". The Guardian (UK), [17 04 2007]; Smitka, M., "Japanese macroeconomic dilemmas: The implications of demographics for growth and stability", Columbia University Academic Commons, [2006]; Demographic Comparison — Switzerland & Japan; Business, Society and Governance in Shrinking Societies: Four Levers of Action for Japan and Switzerland (J. Huber & H. Groth, The Geneva Association, February 2013); H. Groth, Lecture OECD APEC Conference, Tokyo, [14 09 2012]; "Europe's Aging Population Faces Social Problems Similar to Japan's". Asian American Daily, [15 12 2007]; Traphagan, J., W. (2003). Demographic Change and the Family in Japan's Aging Society. SUNY Series in Japan in Transition, SUNY Series in Aging and Culture, p. 16.[2006]; Hewitt, P., (2002). "Depopulation and Ageing in Europe and Japan: The Hazardous Transition to a Labor Shortage Economy". International Politics and Society.

[5] "Abenomics," the stimulus-oriented economic program put forward by Prime Minister Shinzô Abe, had many admirers in the United States, especially among neoKeynesian economistc. Paul Krugman, holding up Abenomics as a model, described Japan's policy as the only operating alternative to the "economic defeatism" of the West: "Nobody else in the advanced world is trying anything similar," he wrote, though he was cautious, offering his judgment on it as "So far, so good." Matt Yglesias, identifying "important lessons for us," declared that Abenomics "seems to be working" and praised Abe for having "brushed off the doubters and plunged ahead with new fiscal stimulus," "leading the path forward to recovery." Mr. Yglesias's headline writers were even more confident than he was: Slate heralded the "Triumph of Abenomics," called it "The Salvation of Japan," and eschewed caution almost entirely: "Prime Minister Shinzo Abe's bold recovery strategy is working." Adam Posen of the Peterson Institute for International Economics, in a generally positive assessment of Abenomics, argued in that Japan should incorporate an even steeper increase in its consumption tax: "Raising the consumption tax to 10 percent, and dangerously suggesting that it might be postponed, is not sufficient. There needs to be a multi-year commitment to raising the consumption tax to the neighborhood of 20 percent." Mr. Posen has an interesting take on the conflicting views about Japanese economic policy: The Abe-doubters, he said, are "leftovers," people without sufficient intellectual talent to have moved on to greener pastures as demand for Japan experts subsided in recent decades. In 2015 P. Krugman moved to group of economists who expressed doubts about the three arrows. In the same group is J. Koll, "Abenomics", ACCJ Journal, December 2013. Most vocal supporters of Abenomics in Japan include Haruhiko Kuroda, governor of Bank of Japan, Koichi Hamada advisor to S. Abe, Motoshige Itoh, University of Tokyo, see his lecture on "Why Abenomics Matters?", Hong Kong Economic Forum, 25 03 2014.

[6] For introduction to Abecomics see, "Definition of Abenomics". Financial Times Lexicon. 28 January 2014; Tax Hike Will Put Abenomics To The Test International, Forbes, 10 01 2013; Kuroda leads Japan down Bernanke's path of escalated easing, Bloomberg, 05 04 2013; Kuroda leads Japan down Bernanke's path of escalated easing Bloomberg 05 04 2013; Behind Abe's Wage Push: Dueling Economists, The Wall Street Journal, 12 03 2014; "Japan's Central-Bank Chief Defends Consumption-Tax Rise", The Wall Street Journal, 14 03 2014.

[7] This is, by the way, what a lot of the commentary has been focused on. The first two arrows have their

detractors from the academic and news worlds, but the third runs up against vested interest groups such as Japan Agriculture and the doctor's union. In addition, it's not going to be easy to change cultural norms regarding the status of women. The success or failure of the third arrow will largely depend on how much the government bows to these groups' interests and successfully causes societal change

For discussion of yed depreciation and trade balance see Wiersum, M., Does Abenomics mean a new era of yen depreciation?, Market Realist, 23 08 2013; Abenomics, Yen Depreciation, Trade Deficit and Export Competitiveness, Shimizu, J., and Sato, K., Discussion Papers from Research Institute of Economy, Trade and Industry (RIETI), [2014]; Is Abenomics' success due to weaker YEN/USD exchange rate (as suggested by Big Mac Index) by Egawa, A., in Improving Economic Policy No.10. [23 07 2013]; del Rosario, K., "Abenomics and the Generic Threat". 15 08 2013; "Over 70% of Japanese not feeling benefits of Abenomics". AFP. 27 01 2014; Another austerity victim: Japan falls back into recession by M. O'Brien M., The Washington Post, 17 11 2014; Weaker than it looks, The Economist, 11 10 2014; Behind Abe's Wage Push: Dueling Economists, The Wall Street Journal, 12 03 2014; Japan: Is That Really The Third Arrow? Does the third arrow of "Abenomics" miss the target in ending Japan's stagnation By Holger Schmieding, The Wall Street Journal 17 06 2013.

[8] The group of prominent economists who express serious criticism about Abenomics include among others, Martin Feldstein, "The Wrong Growth Strategy for Japan", Project Syndicate, 13 10 2013; Richard Katz, "Vooodoo Abenomics", Foreign Affairs, [July/August 2014]; L. Summers and Joseph Stiglitz as well as P. Sheard, Chief Economist for Standard and Poor, "Giving up on Abenomics", Forbes, 24 08 2015. See also Bowles, J., The Absurdity of 'Abenomics' and the PM's 'Three Bendy Arrows' (Part 4: Bubble Economics), The Rationalpessimist.com, 13 05 2015. In total, the BOJ has purchased assets worth ¥150 trillion ($1.3 trillion) in the period of 2012-2014, a 124% increase since the pre-Kuroda level. The BOJ's balance sheet assets are equal to 66% of Japan's GDP, well above the peak levels for other major central banks engaged in easing programs. The bank has purchased almost all new Japanese government bonds sold by Tokyo recently. Critics say that these actions would disrupt market activities and risks being regarded as funding the government debt at rock-bottom level. See, The Truth about Abenomics, The Japanese Economic Experiment That's Captivating The World, by M. Boesler more;

http://www.businessinsider.com/what-is-abenomics-2013-3#ixzz3ccoobWZF; Deflation in Japan, Abenomics and lessons for the euro area, Boeckx, J., Butzen, P., Cordemans, N., Ide, S.; Economic Review, [June 2015]. Also, Grimes, William W. "Will Abenomics Restore Japanese Growth?", National Bureau of Asian Research, [June 2013]. On the merits of yen depreciation compare: Abenomics, Yen Depreciation, Trade Deficit and Export Competitiveness; Shimizu, J., Sato, K., Research Institute of Economy and Trade, Discussion Paper, [2015].; Sakuma, K., "Abenomics and the Value of the Yen", Institute for International Monetary Affairs Newsletter, February 2013; Abenomics propels yen weakness, Ross, Alice, in London, Mackenzie, Michael in New York and Soble, Jonathan in Tokyo, Financial Times , 10 05 2013, see;

http://www.ft.com/intl/cms/s/0/dbdc8d5c-b8d9-11e2-869f-00144feabdc0.html#axzz3cctucqhg

[9] Disenchantment is already appearing in Japan's stock market, which rose by 65% from Abe's ascension until the end of 2013 - almost entirely on buying by foreign investors - but had lost a third of

those gains as foreign investors sold previously purchased assets. These investors feared that Abe is not spending his political clout on reform. Since many Japanese voters view the stock market as the smart money's verdict on revival, if shocks on the exchange continue, that could reduce Abe's approval ratings and his political clout. If Abe is unwilling to take on vested interests to advance reform now, it is hard to see how he will be able to do so after his arguments became weaker.

On relationship between consumer tax increase, inflation and growth see, Szu Ping Chan, "'Godfather' of Abenomics: Japan's sales tax hike must be delayed", The Telegraph, 15 11 2015; Nakamichi, T., "Japan's Tax Increase Puts Abenomics at Risk", Wall Street Journal, 29 08 2014; Komine, T., "Abenomics Has Entered the Second Stage", Japan Foreign Policy Forum, 30 10 2014; Overholdt, W., "Abenomics' Worsening Gamble", Fung Global Institute, Discussion Paper, 18 11 2014.

[10] The issue of the income and the mechanical effect of depreciation is widely explained in textbooks of Macroeconomics. See for example Obstfeld M., Macroeconomics in Open Economy, NY, various editions.

[11] Although it is less known outside Japan than the deflationist episode, a major feature of the Lost Decade is the productivity slowdown at the aggregate level, which has been the focus of a lively academic debate in Japan. Between 1995 and 2004, the annual average gross value added growth has been 0.7% in Japan against 3.7% in the US, with a contribution of TFP growth of 0.4% and 1.7% respectively, whereas during the period 1980-1995 gross value added growth was 3.6% in Japan and 2.9% in the US with a contribution of TFP growth of 1.2% and 0.5% respectively. See Fukao, K. and others in "Productivity in Japan, the US, and the major EU economies: Is Japan Falling Behind?", RIETI Discussion Paper Series 07-E-046, 30 07 2007.

[12] There are already many scenarios of the emerging financial collapse in Japan ranging from realistic prognoses to very dramatic and more problematic outcomes. Among the former ones is in "the Next Currency Set to Fail" in Global Economy, 27 03 2015 by J. Opdyke.

[13] See for example, "What Model for Japan's Future? Overcoming the Hollowing-out Syndrome". Presentation at the Brookings Institution Conference on "the Hollowing-Out of Japan's Economy: myths, Facts, Countermeasures", 20 02 2013 by Jun Saito from Keio University.

[14] On income and "mechanical" effects of currency depreciation see R. v. Dornbush, "Open Market Macroeconomics". Princeton Press, various editions. The author points out, along with other economists, that using currency depreciation for improving terms of trade is usually a counterproductive measure.

[15] Keynesian multiplier for Japan is estimated to be between 0.5% to 1.7%. See Roberts, M., Blogging form Marxist economist, The smugness multiplier, [October 2012], Also by the same author, What's wrong with the Keynesian answer to austerity?, Socialist Review, [April 2013].

[16] Reinhart, C.M. and Kenneth S. Rogoff, Growth in a Time of Debt, American Economic Review: Papers & Proceedings: 573–578, No 5, [2010].

[17] Reinhart, Carmen M., and Kenneth S. Rogoff. "The Aftermath of Financial Crises." American Economic Review, 99(2): 466–72[2009]; Barro, Robert J., "On the Determination of the Public Debt", The Journal of Political Economy, Vol. 85, No. 5: 940-971[1979]; Olivier, Jeanne and Gucina, Anastasia, "Government Debt in Emerging Market Countries: A New Data Set", International Monetary Fund Working Paper 6/98. Washington DC, [2006]; Calvo, Guillermo, A., Alejandro, Izquierdo, and

Rudy, Loo-Kung, "Relative Price Volatility Under Sudden Stops: The Relevance of Balance Sheet Effects", Journal of International Economics Vol. 9, No. 1: 231–254[2006]. For other views see, Herndon, Thomas, Ash, Michael, Pollin, Robert, "Does High Public Debt Consistently Stifle Economic Growth? A Critique of Reinhart and Rogoff", Political Economy Research Institute, University of Massachusetts Amherst, [15 04 2013]; Shuchman, Daniel, (18 04 2013). "That Reinhart and Rogoff Committed a Spreadsheet Error Completely Misses the Point". Capital Flows, Forbes.com.; Smith, Jeremy (20 04 2013). "From Reinhart & Rogoff's Own Data: UK GDP Increased Fastest When Debt-to-GDP Ratio Was Highest and the Debt Ratio Came Down!". Prime: Policy Research in Macroeconomics, Policy Research in Macroeconomics, (17 04 2013); "George Osborne's Favourite 'Godfathers of Austerity' Economists Admit to Making Error in Research". Mirror Online in Business Insider Newsletter, BNP ECONOMIST.com; Japan's 'Abenomics' Experiment Will End In Tears In 2015, by Matthew Boesler, 14 02 2013.

[18] Inflation forecasts for Japan, see G20 Economic Forecast in
<http://knoema.com/chjehcb/japan-inflator>

[19] According to Asahi Shimbun Poll, 20 01 2015, 53% of the population expressed pessimism about Abenomics, 63% regarded last election as useless and waste of time. According to the earlier Pew Global Research Survey, May 2013, over 70% of the Japanese do not expect any improvement in national economy in future and 73 % believed that economy was not doing well. According to Japan Today poll, 28 01 2014, over 70 % of Japanese do not feel any improvement because of Abenomics. See also, Richard Katz' paper, "Voodoo Economics Japan's Failed Plan", Katz, R., Foreign Affairs, [July/August 2014].

Chapter 3

Health and Consumer Behavior

Hiroaki Teramoto
Faculty of Economic Sciences, Hiroshima Shudo University
1-1 Ozuka-Higashi 1-chome, Asaminami-ku, Hiroshima, JAPAN 731-3195

Abstract

I introduce and consider three representative articles on health economics, particularly medical expenditure. A consumer's behavior is affected by his or her level of health. If one's health declines (illness), the consumer changes his or her behavior. In industrialized countries or aging societies, overall expenditure for medical care is increasing and becoming an imminent problem. The field of economics has a significant amount of research on this field, some of which was reviewed for this study. The first two studies on cost-effective analysis were by Garber and Phelps [8], and Meltzer [14]. The third study is the work of Graff Zivin and Neidell [10], who analyzed the effects of medical care when environmental pollution occurs. These three works depend on the consumer's (expected) utility maximization.

I believe that these three studies are pioneering in their field and deserve introduction and consideration.

Key Words:
Health economics, Medical care, Cost-effectiveness analysis, Lifetime utility maximization, Quality adjusted life year, Future costs, Health production function

1. Introduction

A consumer attempts to maximize his or her utility subject to budget constraints. This behavior occurs for a certain health condition. Therefore, when a consumer's health condition changes, his or her behavior changes accordingly. If the consumer becomes richer or older, he or she may increase his or her health expenditures [1]. If the health condition becomes serious, the consumer's behavior may change completely, and the behavior of individuals around him or her may be significantly affected. This

---
[1] See, Hall and Jones [12]. The overall study on the increase of health care spending is summarized by Chernew and Newhouse [3].

situation explains the need for a microeconomic analysis of consumer health [2].

In this era of international exchange and a global economy, occurrences such as infectious diseases and the outbreak of pandemics considerably influence consumer behavior [3]. Consequently, medical service expenditure is expected to increase considerably. Alternatively, as wealthier people age, they are said to have incentives to spend their money or fortunes on health or anti-aging measures. In addition, when a nation or a society ages rapidly, the shape and level of the consumption function changes and the rate of medical expenditures over gross domestic product (GDP), as well as the total amount of medical expenditures, continuously increases. Macroeconomic analysis and explanations are needed for such situations.

In recent years, many economic studies on medical care have been conducted [4]. I introduce and consider some of the significant articles on consumer behavior.

2. Analysis of Cost-effectiveness in Medical Care

A consumer receives medical treatment when he or she desires. In this sense, whether or how much to receive is a consumer utility maximization problem. However, from the standpoint of the socially optimal consumption level of medical care, the consumer's individual utility maximization is insufficient. Meltzer and Smith [15] note that a large part of health care is financed not individually but collectively, which tends to cause excess consumption. For such a situation, one of the most appropriate approaches is the cost-benefit analysis (CBA). This analysis has been applied primarily to the project evaluation of the public sector and has obtained good results. Therefore, that CBA should be applied to the field of medical care is natural. However, Meltzer and Smith explain that because a monetary evaluation of the health condition is inevitably ambiguous, a different or a qualitative approach that does not use such an evaluation may be superior. In this sense, a cost-effectiveness analysis (CEA) is relevant. Currently, a CEA for medical care is considered one of the most superior tools in health economics and is applied to many fields [5].

2.1. Quality Adjusted Life Year and CEA

Garber and Phelps [8] consider the problem of evaluating medical interventions in an intertemporal setting. The interventions are assumed to have differing effects on all future period survival probabilities, and they also consider the concept of quality of life. Their analysis is done in the framework of maximization of expected utility, and optimal solutions are obtained to form a solid basis

---

[2] Murphy and Topel [16] emphasize the importance of medical research from the standpoint of economics.
[3] With regard to the economic analysis of a flu epidemic or pandemic, see, Almond and Mazumber [2], and Almond [1].
[4] To take a general view of this, see, for example, Culyer and Newhouse [5], Phelps [19], and Pauly, McGuire and Barros [18].
[5] Meltzer explains the medical cost-effectiveness analysis as follows: "Medical cost-effectiveness analysis is intended to provide a guide for choosing among potential medical interventions in order to achieve the best possible outcomes given the available resources." See Meltzer [14], (p.33). About the theoretical appraisal of CEA, see Weinstein and Manning [20].

for subsequent studies[6]. I introduce their model.

Garber and Phelps suppose two medical interventions, a and b, each of which has the ability to alter quality of life and the possibility of future survival. They define the notion of the Quality Adjusted Life Year (QALY) as follows: P_j is the probability that a person alive during the preceding period will be alive in period j. Then, the cumulative probability F_i that a person is alive in period i is shown as:

$$F_i = \prod_{j=1}^{i} P_j \tag{2.1.1}$$

Garber and Phelps express the expected QALY value as:

$$\text{QALY} = \sum_{i=1}^{N} F_i \delta^i k_i \tag{2.1.2}$$

Regarding expression (2.1.2), N is the maximum life span, δ is a time discount factor and is shown as $\delta = 1/(1+r)$, where r is a discount rate, and k_i represents the quality adjustment, the value of which ranges from zero (the worst state of health, i.e., death or its equivalent) to 1 (perfect health). The term k involves general aspects of quality of life and k_i is the expected value of the quality adjustment for all possible states of health in period i.

By adding the concept of QALY, Garber and Phelps consider the utility maximization problem. The lifetime expected utility $E_0 U$, which is viewed from time 0, is shown as:

$$E_0 U = U_0(Y - w_a a - w_b b) + \sum_{i=1}^{N} U_i(Y_i) F_i \tag{2.1.3}$$

where w_a and w_b are the unit cost of the medical interventions a and b respectively.

The utility U_i in period i is expressed as $U_i = v \delta^i k_i$, where $v = U_0(Y)$ and income Y is measured in real terms and assumed to be constant over time. The expected utility is rewritten as:

$$E_0 U = U_0(Y - w_a a - w_b b) + v \sum_{i=1}^{N} \left[\delta^i k_i \prod_{j=1}^{i} P_j \right] \tag{2.1.4}$$

where $\sum_{i=1}^{N} \left[\delta^i k_i \prod_{j=1}^{i} P_j \right]$ is the value of QALY remaining as of period 1. $dU_0(Y - w_a a - w_b b)/dY$ is denoted as U_0'.

The two medical interventions, a and b, affect the survival probability P_i and the expected quality adjustment k_i in future period i. Garber and Phelps define $\partial P_i / \partial a = \epsilon_i^a$, $\partial P_i / \partial b = \epsilon_i^b$, $\partial k_i / \partial a = \psi_i^a$, $\partial k_i / \partial b = \psi_i^b$, and $V_i = k_i F_i$. To obtain the optimal value of a, equation (2.1.4) is differentiated with respect to a, that is:

$$\frac{\partial E_0 U}{\partial a} = -w_a U_0' + v \sum_{i=1}^{N} \delta^i \frac{\partial V_i}{\partial a} \tag{2.1.5}$$

Garber and Phelps explain equation (2.1.5) as follows. The left-hand side of equation (2.1.5) expresses the change in expected utility resulting from a change in medical intervention a. The first term of the right-hand side expresses the expenditure-induced loss of period 0 utility and the second term expresses the gain in future (that is from period 1 to N) expected utility. Regarding the derivative of V_i, the following equation is shown, that is:

$$\frac{\partial V_i}{\partial a} = \psi_i^a F_i + k_i \frac{\partial F_i}{\partial a} \tag{2.1.6}$$

---

[6] Garber [6] and Garber and Sculpher [7] study and explain the development of cost-effectiveness analysis in health care. The former includes the central contents of the Garber and Phelps model and shows the medical decision-making function. The latter, in a comparison using cost-benefit analysis, explains how cost-effectiveness analysis is used in the domain of coverage and payment policies. These two studies, as well as the Garber and Phelps model, give us a clear understanding of CEA.

The left-hand side of equation (2.1.6) is the change in expected utility in period i resulting from the change in a. The first term of the right-hand side is the change in the quality factor expected in period i multiplied by the probability of being alive then. The second term is the change in the survival probability multiplied by the expected utility. By using equation (2.1.6) and the definition of survival probability, equation (2.1.5) is revised as [7]:

$$\frac{\partial E_0 U}{\partial a} = -w_a U_0' + v \left\{ \sum_{i=1}^{N} \delta^i \prod_{j=1}^{i} P_j \left(\psi_i^a + k_i \sum_{k=1}^{i} \frac{\epsilon_k^a}{P_k} \right) \right\} \quad (2.1.7)$$

At the optimum, the value of equation (2.1.7) is set to zero. A similar relationship holds for intervention b. Garber and Phelps point out that utility is a function of discounted QALY and the term in braces, that is:

$$\sum_{i=1}^{N} \delta^i \prod_{j=1}^{i} P_j \left(\psi_i^a + k_i \sum_{k=1}^{i} \frac{\epsilon_k^a}{P_k} \right) \quad (2.1.8)$$

expresses the incremental effect of a on QALYs. They denote this term as $\partial Q/\partial a$ and emphasize that it has central significance.

From equation (2.1.7), the optimal level of investment in the medical intervention a is shown as:

$$w_a = \frac{v}{U_0'} \frac{\partial Q}{\partial a} = \frac{v}{U_0'} \left\{ \sum_{i=1}^{N} \delta^i \prod_{j=1}^{i} P_j \left(\psi_i^a + k_i \sum_{k=1}^{i} \frac{\epsilon_k^a}{P_k} \right) \right\} \quad (2.1.9)$$

Regarding (2.1.9), Garber and Phelps explain that the marginal benefit of medical care is the scaled utility (v/U_0') of the incremental QALYs from incremental a and, at the optimum, marginal benefit $(v/U_0')(\partial Q/\partial a)$ is equal to marginal cost w_a. A similar argument holds for medical intervention b.

The previous discussion represents the introduction of a portion of the Garber and Phelps model. I now consider the characteristics of their model.

First, different from many cost-benefit analysis studies, Garber and Phelps consider the change in quality of life and life expectancy caused by medical intervention. This consideration is an advantage of CEA. They adopt the QALY (QALY $= \sum_{i=1}^{N} F_i \delta^i k_i$) index. Because this index is composed of the (cumulative) probability of survival, a time discount factor, and a quality adjustment, QALY has a considerable degree of objectivity. This index is not evaluated using a money term but instead using quality, which is suitable to the CEA. However, I must stress that, even though the index is qualitative, it cannot escape subjectivity because its constituents are evaluated using not monetary terms but an estimation that, to some extent, involves subjectivity.

Second, Garber and Phelps derived the conditions for optimal levels of medical interventions a and b. The optimal condition for a indicates that the marginal benefit $((U/U_0')(\partial Q/\partial a))$ of a is equal

---

[7] With regard to the equation (2.1.7), this is derived as follows,

$$\frac{\partial V_i}{\partial a} = \frac{\partial (k_i F_i)}{\partial a} = \frac{\partial k_i}{\partial a} F_i + k_i \frac{\partial F_i}{\partial a} = \frac{\partial k_i}{\partial a} P_1 P_2 \cdots P_i + k_i \frac{\partial (P_1 P_2 \cdots P_i)}{\partial a}$$

$$= \frac{\partial k_i}{\partial a} P_1 P_2 \cdots P_i + k_i \left(\frac{\partial P_1}{\partial a} P_2 P_3 \cdots P_i + P_1 \frac{\partial P_2}{\partial a} P_3 \cdots P_i + \cdots + P_1 \cdots P_{i-1} \frac{\partial P_i}{\partial a} \right)$$

$$= \frac{\partial k_i}{\partial a} P_1 P_2 \cdots P_i + k_i \left(\frac{\partial P_1}{\partial a}/P_1 + \frac{\partial P_2}{\partial a}/P_2 + \cdots + \frac{\partial P_i}{\partial a}/P_i \right) P_1 P_2 \cdots P_i$$

$$= \frac{\partial k_i}{\partial a} \prod_{j=1}^{i} P_j + k_i \sum_{k=1}^{i} \left(\frac{\partial P_k}{\partial a}/P_k \right) \prod_{j=1}^{n} P_j = \prod_{j=1}^{i} P_j \left(\psi_i^a + k_i \sum_{k=1}^{i} \frac{\epsilon_k^a}{P_k} \right)$$

where, as is shown before, $\psi_i^a = \partial k_i/\partial a$ and $\epsilon_i^a = \partial P_i/\partial a$. By substituting this relationship into the equation (2.1.5), the equation (2.1.7) is obtained.

to its marginal cost (w_a). Marginal benefit involves the effect of additional medical intervention a on the QALYs. The Garber and Phelps model shows two effects of a on the QALYs—survival probability and expected quality adjustment—thus indicating the original and significant characteristics of their model.

2.2. Future Costs in CEA

In cost-effectiveness analyses, the formulation of expenditures is important. Is the expenditure for the specific and related illness or for health in general? Moreover, is that effect a one-time occurrence or cumulative? Alternatively, does the expenditure have the effect of prolonging life? Numerous analyses attempt to answer these questions. Among these, Meltzer [14] considers both future and present costs and expresses their cumulative effects. His analysis is one of the representative works on CEA[8]. I introduce his model.

Meltzer uses the concept of expected utility to analyze the effects of changing medical expenditures on lifetime utility. The lifetime expected EU of a consumer is formulated as:

$$EU = \sum_{t=1}^{T} \beta^t S_t U_t \qquad (2.2.1)$$

where β^t is a time preference discount factor $(\beta < 1)$, S_t is the probability of surviving to time t, and U_t is the utility at time t.

Medical interventions have two effects on lifetime utility. One effect is survival probabilities and the other effect is on utility by improving health. Therefore, the probability S_t of survival to time t is assumed to depend upon all past possible medical interventions in each period, that is, $S_t = S_t(m_{11}, \cdots, m_{Kt-1})$, where m_{kt} represents the expenditure on medical intervention k at time t. Regarding utility U_t at time t, Meltzer assumes that it depends on both consumption c_t and health H_t at time t. Regarding H_t, because the health condition at time t is considered to depend on past expenditures on health, the relationship $H_t = H_t(m_{11}, \cdots, m_{Kt-1})$ is assumed to hold. Then, the utility function U_t is expressed as $U_t = U_t(c_t, H_t(m_{11}, \cdots, m_{Kt-1}))$.

In explaining these assumptions, Meltzer specifies the expected lifetime utility as follows:

$$EU = \sum_{t=1}^{T} \beta^t S_t(m_{11}, \cdots, m_{Kt-1}) U_t(c_t, H_t(m_{11}, \cdots, m_{Kt-1})) \qquad (2.2.2)$$

Then, the lifetime budget constraint of the person is specified. Taking into account the assumption that the probability S_t of the person being alive at time t depends on past expenditure $m_{k\tau}(k = 1, \cdots, K: \tau = 1, \cdots, t-1)$, that is, $S_t = S_t(m_{11}, \cdots, m_{Kt-1})$, the lifetime budget constraint is specified as:

$$\sum_{t=1}^{T} [1/(1+r)]^t S_t(m_{11}, \cdots, m_{Kt-1})(c_t + m_{kt})$$
$$= \sum_{t=1}^{T} [1/(1+r)]^t S_t(m_{11}, \cdots, m_{Kt-1}) i_t \qquad (2.2.3)$$

The left-hand side of expression (2.2.3) is the person's expected level of expenditures and the right-hand side is his or her expected budget (resources). The symbol r is the interest rate, $1/(1+r)$ is a discount factor, and i_t is the earned income at time t.

---

[8] Meltzer and Smith [15] point out that "medical CEA is perhaps the most widely applied tool to guide policy decisions" (p. 434). Their summary of the models on individual utility maximization and CEA includes the Meltzer model that we intend to introduce. Their work forms a broad basis for the future development of the analysis.

Meltzer formulates the problem that maximizes the expected lifetime utility (2.2.2) subject to the lifetime budget constraint (2.2.3). The first-order conditions for consumption c_t and medical care m_{it} are shown as:

$$\beta^t S_t(m_{11},\cdots,m_{Kt-1}) \frac{\partial U_t(c_t, H_t(m_{11},\cdots,m_{Kt-1}))}{\partial c_t}$$
$$= \lambda\{(1/(1+r))^t S_t(m_{11},\cdots,m_{Kt-1})\} \quad t=1,\cdots,T \quad (2.2.4)$$

$$\sum_{\tau=1}^{T} \beta^\tau \left[\frac{\partial S_\tau(m_{11},\cdots,m_{K\tau-1})}{\partial m_{it}}\right] U_\tau(c_\tau, H_\tau(m_{11},\cdots,m_{K\tau-1}))$$
$$+ S_\tau(m_{11},\cdots,m_{K\tau-1}) \frac{\partial U_\tau(c_\tau, H_\tau(m_{11},\cdots,m_{K\tau-1}))}{\partial m_{it}}$$
$$= \lambda\{(1/(1+r))^t S_t(m_{11},\cdots,m_{K\tau-1}) + \sum_{\tau=t}^{T}(1/(1+r))^\tau$$
$$\times \left[\frac{\partial S_\tau(m_{11},\cdots,m_{K\tau-1})}{\partial m_{it}}\left[c_\tau + \sum_{j=1}^{K} m_{j\tau} - i_\tau\right]\right]\} \quad i=1,\cdots,k,\ t=1,\cdots,T \quad (2.2.5)$$

The optimal condition (2.2.4) indicates that the discounted expected marginal utility of consumption at each age is equal to the discounted expected cost. The interpretation of the optimal condition (2.2.5) is somewhat complex. Medical intervention has two effects expected utility, that is, the effect on the change in the survival probability and the effect on the change in health during a lifetime. Similarly, the cost side consists of two parts: the direct cost of the medical intervention and the effect on net expenditures as generated by the change in survival probabilities. Note that the terms for expressions (2.2.4) and (2.2.5) are discounted values.

To conduct the cost-effectiveness analysis, Meltzer rearranges the optimal condition concerning medical expenditures (2.2.5) as follows:

$$\frac{[1/(1+r)]^t S_t(m_{K\tau-1}) + \sum_{\tau=t}^{T}[1/(1+r)]^\tau \left[\partial S_\tau(m_{K\tau-1})/\partial m_{it}\left[c_\tau + \sum_{j=1}^{K} m_{j\tau} - i_\tau\right]\right]}{\sum_{\tau=t}^{T} \beta^\tau \left[[\partial S_\tau(m_{K\tau-1})/\partial m_{it}] U_\tau(c_\tau, H_\tau(m_{K\tau-1})) + S_\tau(m_{K\tau-1})[\partial U_\tau(c_\tau, H_\tau(m_{K\tau-1}))/\partial m_{it}]\right]}$$
$$= 1/\lambda \quad i=1,\cdots,K, t=1,\cdots,T \quad (2.2.6)$$

where $m_{K\tau-1} = (m_{11},\cdots,m_{K T-1})$. Equation (2.2.6) indicates that, for the optimization of medical expenditure, the ratio of marginal cost to marginal benefit of all medical interventions should be equal to the reciprocal of λ, or $1/\lambda$, where λ is a Lagrange multiplier and represents the marginal utility of income [9].

---

[9] Similarly, the optimal condition concerning consumption (2.2.4) are rearranged as:
$$\frac{(1/(1+r))^t S_t(m_{11},\cdots,m_{Kt-1})}{\beta^t S_t(m_{11},\cdots,m_{Kt-1}) \frac{\partial U_t(c_t, H_t(m_{11},\cdots,m_{Kt-1}))}{\partial c_t}} = \frac{1}{\lambda}$$

The interpretation should be done similarly and from these I see that the following relationship holds:

$$\frac{\beta^t S_t(m_{11},\cdots,m_{Kt-1}) \frac{\partial U_t(c_t, H_t(m_{11},\cdots,m_{Kt-1}))}{\partial c_t}}{\sum_{\tau=1}^{T} \beta^\tau \left[\frac{\partial S_\tau(m_{11},\cdots,m_{K\tau-1})}{\partial m_{it}}\right] U_\tau(c_\tau, H_\tau(m_{11},\cdots,m_{K\tau-1})) + S_\tau(m_{11},\cdots,m_{K\tau-1}) \frac{\partial U_\tau(c_\tau, H_\tau(m_{11},\cdots,m_{K\tau-1}))}{\partial m_{it}}}$$
$$= \frac{(1/(1+r))^t S_t(m_{11},\cdots,m_{Kt-1})}{(1/(1+r))^t S_t(m_{11},\cdots,m_{K\tau-1}) + \sum_{\tau=t}^{T}(1/(1+r))^\tau \left[\frac{\partial S_\tau(m_{11},\cdots,m_{K\tau-1})}{\partial m_{it}}\left[c_\tau + \sum_{j=1}^{K} m_{j\tau} - i_\tau\right]\right]}$$

This relationship means that the marginal rate of substitution between medical intervention m_{it} and consumption c_t is equal to its relative (shadow) price. I see that the optimal conditions (2.2.4) and (2.2.5) have the standard

The previous discussion represents the introduction of a portion of the Meltzer model. I now consider the characteristics of his model.

First, Meltzer formulates that the effects of medical interventions are twofold: effects on survival probability and effects on utility from improving health. The effect on survival probability has considerable similarity to the model of Garber and Phelps and constitutes a significant element of the effect of medical interventions.

Second, the advantage of Meltzer model is that consumer's time allocation is introduce to his cost-effectiveness analysis. Indeed, instead of the formulation of the expected lifetime utility function (2.2.1) or (2.2.2), Meltzer show the reformulated utility function as: $EU = \sum_{t=1}^{T} \beta^t S_t(m_{11}, \cdots, m_{Kt-1}) U_t(c_t, l_t, H_t(m_{11}, \cdots, m_{Kt-1}))$, where l_t is the leisure time. Using this function and revised budget constraint which involves earned income, Meltzer derived the optimal conditions. Though these conditions are similar to those without time allocation, it have the possibility to extend the model [10].

Third, Meltzer shows that utility at time t depends on both consumption and health at time t. Health at time t is assumed to depend on past expenditures on health. I believe that this assumption is persuasive and contributes to the fruitfulness of Meltzer's model. However, I also believe that this assumption can be improved. If the health condition at time t depends on past consumption and past expenditures on health, the revised function $h_t = h_t(m_{11}, \cdots, m_{Kt-1}: c_1, \cdots, c_{t-1})$ holds instead of the original function $H_t = H_t(m_{11}, \cdots, m_{Kt-1})$. If this condition is true, then the optimal condition may be revised slightly [11]. However, this point is minor and I believe that the Meltzer model is a path-breaking and influential model in medical intervention analysis.

3. Pollution and Health Production

Typically, a consumer spends his or her income on medical care and goods and services. Medical

---

property of microeconomics.

[10] In this paper, I explained the Meltzer's basic model to introduce the essences of his model. The Meltzer model which involves time allocation is a little complex. But the interpretation of the results is similar.

[11] In this situation, the optimal condition (2.2.4) may be revised as

$$\beta^t S_t(m_{11}, \cdots, m_{Kt-1}) \left[\frac{\partial U_t(c_t, h_t(m_{11}, \cdots, m_{Kt-1}: c_1, \cdots, c_{t-1}))}{\partial c_t} \right.$$
$$\left. + \frac{\partial U_t(c_t, h_t(m_{11}, \cdots, m_{Kt-1}: c_1, \cdots, c_{t-1}))}{\partial h_t(m_{11}, \cdots, m_{Kt-1}: c_1, \cdots, c_{t-1})} \frac{\partial h_t(m_{11}, \cdots, m_{Kt-1}: c_1, \cdots, c_{t-1})}{\partial c_t} \right]$$
$$= \lambda \{(1/(1+r))^t S_t(m_{11}, \cdots, m_{Kt-1})$$

With regard to this optimal equation, the first term $\partial U_t / \partial c_t$ expresses the marginal utility of consumption, and the second term $(\partial U_t / \partial h_t)(\partial h_t / \partial c_t)$ can be interpreted separately, that is, $\partial U_t / \partial h_t$ expresses the marginal utility of health, and $\partial h_t / \partial c_t$ expresses the rate of increment of health over the increment of consumption—interpreted as the additional consumption effects on health. In summary, the second term $(\partial U_t / \partial h_t)(\partial h_t / \partial c_t)$ expresses the effect of consumption on utility through the health condition. I must point out that the sign of $(\partial h_t / \partial c_t)$ is not always positive. Certain types or manners of consumption are known to have harmful effects on a consumer's health. In this case, the sign of $(\partial h_t / \partial c_t)$ is negative. In industrialized countries, because consumption goods are affluent, how much to take or what to choose are, in some cases, essential to health. Alternatively, in developing countries, if people consume inferior quality goods because of small budgets, such consumption does not contribute to their health. If the functions H_t and U_t are revised, other related expressions and (2.2.4) must also be revised.

care is demanded for the prevention and treatment of diseases. Additionally, if the consumer suffers from environmental pollution, remedies must be taken to maintain one's health condition and ability to supply labor. In the economic literature, the theory of human capital may be one of the most suitable analytical tools. Grossman [11] proposes the concept of health capital, which has essential effects on the economic analysis of health. Health is not a given but is successively formed by the consumer. At the same time, Grossman points out that health capital influences the consumer's supply of labor. Based on the work of Grossman, Harrington and Portney [13], Cropper and Freeman III [4] and Graff Zivin and Neidell [10] propose in their review article a health production function that indicates the consumer's efforts to avoid the negative influence of pollution and to recover one's health. I believe that their article makes a considerable contribution to health economics. Next, I introduce the Graff Zivin and Neidell model [12].

Graff Zivin and Neidell formulate the health production function of a representative person. They suppose that the person is exposed to pollution and that the pollution is mitigated by avoidance behavior. Moreover, medical care is used to ameliorate the negative health effects of pollution. Then, the health production function H is shown as:

$$H = H(P, M, A) \tag{3.1}$$

where P is ambient pollution levels, A is avoidance behavior to mitigate the influence of pollution, and M is medical care to ameliorate medical conditions. Of these variables, Graff Zivin and Neidell explain that avoidance behavior is a preventive measure and medical care consumption is aftercare for illnesses caused by pollution.

Graff Zivin and Niedell believe that an environmentally driven illness episode ϕ is determined by ambient pollution level P and avoidance behavior A, that is, $\phi = \phi(P, A)$. Medical expenditure M is made according to the extent of illness episode ϕ, that is, $M = M(\phi)$. Then, they reformulate the health production function (3.1) as follows:

$$H = H(M(\phi), \phi(P, A)) \tag{3.2}$$

Concerning this equation, Graff Zivin and Niedell explain that, because medical expenditures are made to reduce the disutility of illness, a person's health H depends on both medical expenditures and illness episodes.

Graff Zivin and Niedell express a person's utility U as depending on health H, consumption X, and leisure L, that is:

$$U = U(X, L, H) \tag{3.3}$$

Graff Zivin and Neidell believe that a person's health condition affects his or her labor productivity and, hence, the extent of wage w, that is, $w = w(H)$. Regarding time allocation, the total available time T is divided between labor hour and leisure L, that is, labor hour $= T - L$. Then, the person's labor income is shown as $w(H)[T - L]$ and non-wage income is denoted as I. In this situation, the person's budget constraint is expressed as:

$$I + w(H)[T - L] = c_X X + c_A A + c_M M \tag{3.4}$$

where $c_j (j = X, A, M)$ denotes the price of good j. Then, the person's utility maximization problem

---

[12] They wrote another article relevant to this. See, Graff Zivin and Neidell [9]. Neidell [17] analyzed the relationship between air pollution and health.

is to maximize (3.3) with regard to the variables $X, L, A,$ and M subject to constraint (3.4), that is:

$$\max_{(X,L,A,M)} \mathcal{L} = U(X, L, H(M(\phi), \phi(P, A)))$$

$$+ \lambda \{I + w(H)[T - L] - c_X X - c_A A - c_M M\} \quad (3.5)$$

Graff Zivin and Neidell derive the first-order optimal condition as follows:

$$\frac{\partial \mathcal{L}}{\partial X} = \frac{\partial U}{\partial X} - \lambda c_X = 0, \qquad \frac{\partial \mathcal{L}}{\partial L} = \frac{\partial U}{\partial L} - \lambda w = 0 \quad (3.6)$$

$$\frac{\partial \mathcal{L}}{\partial A} = \frac{\partial U}{\partial H}\left(\frac{\partial H}{\partial M}\frac{\partial M}{\partial \phi}\frac{\partial \phi}{\partial A} + \frac{\partial H}{\partial \phi}\frac{\partial \phi}{\partial A}\right) - \lambda\left(c_A - \frac{\partial w}{\partial H}\left(\frac{\partial H}{\partial M}\frac{\partial M}{\partial \phi}\frac{\partial \phi}{\partial A} + \frac{\partial H}{\partial \phi}\frac{\partial \phi}{\partial A}\right)[T - L]\right) = 0 \quad (3.7)$$

$$\frac{\partial \mathcal{L}}{\partial M} = \frac{\partial U}{\partial H}\frac{\partial H}{\partial M} - \lambda\left(c_M - \frac{\partial w}{\partial H}\frac{\partial H}{\partial M}[T - L]\right) = 0 \quad (3.8)$$

The two equations for (3.6) express the standard trade-offs between labor and leisure; in other words, the marginal rate of substitution between consumption X and leisure L. That is, $(\partial U/\partial X)/(\partial U/\partial L)$ is equal to its relative price c_X/w. By combining equations (3.7) and (3.8), the following intuitive expression is obtained[13]:

$$\left(\frac{\partial H}{\partial A}\right)/\left(\frac{\partial H}{\partial M}\right) = \frac{c_A}{c_M} \quad (3.9)$$

This expression indicates that avoidance behavior A and medical treatment M should be consumed at the ratio of the marginal productivities of each, and that increasing health H is equal to its relative price.

The previous discussion represents an introduction to the central part of the Graff Zivin and Neidell model. I now consider their model.

First, Graff Zivin and Niedell show the health production function that I believe is exquisitely formulated to explain the behavior of environmental pollution victims. The function involves both the preventive or avoiding measure and the ameliorating measure or aftercare. These two types of measures are effective in expressing the victim's behavior to protect or restore his or her health.

Second, in a sense, it is natural that the economic analysis of health grapples with the relationship between health and labor supply. Graff Zivin and Neidell also analyze this relationship. They connect the health production function and the wage rate using the assumption that the level of wages is a function of the health condition. Therefore, in the context of utility maximization, the health condition (which is assumed to be affected by environmental factors and simultaneously influences the wage rate), consumption level, and leisure time play major roles. I believe that their model is unique and sophisticated and, thus, is a guidepost for subsequent analysts.

---

[13] From equations (3.7) and (3.8), the following expression is obtained:

$$\frac{\frac{\partial U}{\partial H}\left(\frac{\partial H}{\partial M}\frac{\partial M}{\partial \phi}\frac{\partial \phi}{\partial A} + \frac{\partial H}{\partial \phi}\frac{\partial \phi}{\partial A}\right)}{\frac{\partial U}{\partial H}\frac{\partial H}{\partial M}} = \frac{c_A - \frac{\partial w}{\partial H}\left(\frac{\partial H}{\partial M}\frac{\partial M}{\partial \phi}\frac{\partial \phi}{\partial A} + \frac{\partial H}{\partial \phi}\frac{\partial \phi}{\partial A}\right)[T-L]}{c_M - \frac{\partial w}{\partial H}\frac{\partial H}{\partial M}[T-L]}.$$

This equation indicates that the marginal rate of substitution between avoidance behavior and medical treatment is equal to their relative costs.

4. Conclusion

We introduced and considered three studies on health economics and, in particular, medical care. The first and second studies are based on cost-effectiveness analysis (CEA). CEA is one of the most widely adopted approaches in studies on the appraisal of medical expenditures. This analysis intends to evaluate the effects not in monetary terms but in a qualitative context. For example, the effects of medical expenditures are measured by actually or probabilistically prolonged life year, quality of life (QOL), and quality adjusted life years (QALYs). Indeed, these indices exclude the ambiguities caused by a monetary evaluation. I believe with certainty that this quality analysis will continuously develop. However, because this analysis is significantly used in policy evaluations, the monetary evaluation is certainly inevitable. On this point, the evaluation of the elements U/U_0' in equation (2.1.9) and the Lagrange multiplier λ in equations (2.2.4) to (2.2.6) are important.

The third study uses a model based on the health production function. This model indicates that the state of health affects both consumer utility and labor productivity on wage rate. The realistic expression of a consumer's behavior concerning health and earning capacity is sophisticated and persuasive. Moreover, I believe that this model has broad applicability and analyzes the relationship between pollution and health (and avoidance behavior, medical care, labor supply, and utility). Instead, of pollution, this model is able to analyze the effect of the occurrence of infectious disease. Alternatively, with modifications, the model could also analyze the contraction of a chronic disease. Many consumers take care to avoid contracting a chronic disease during middle age, however, some fall ill with such conditions and must receive treatment, possibly hampering their labor productivity and wage rate. Such a situation may concern the individual consumer and may affect the national health care system. In this sense, this model has macroeconomic and microeconomic significance.

In this age of an aging society and a global economy, I believe that economic analyses of health and the health care system are becoming indispensable.

References

[1] Almond, Douglas, "Is the 1918 Influenza Pandemic Over? Long-Term Effects of In Utero Influenza Exposure in the Post-1940 U. S. Population," *Journal of Political Economy* 114 (4), 672-712 (2006).

[2] Almond, Douglas, and Bhashkar Mazumber, "The 1918 Influenza Pandemic and Subsequent Health Outcomes: An Analysis of SIPP Data," *American Economic Review* 95 (2), 258-62 (2005).

[3] Chernew, Michael E., and Joseph P. Newhouse, "Health Care Spending Growth" In, Pauly, Mark V., McGuire, Thomas G. and Barros, Pedro P. (Eds.), Handbook of Health Economics, vol. 2. North-Holland, Amsterdam, 1-43 (2012).

[4] Cropper, Maureen L., and A. Myric Freeman III, "Environmental Health Effects," In: John B. Braden and Charles D. Kolstad (Eds.), *Measuring the Demand for Environmental quality*, Emerald, UK, 165-211 (1991).

[5] Culyer, A. J., and Joseph P. Newhouse (Eds.), Handbook of Health Economics, vol. 1A.

North-Holland, Amsterdam, (2000).

[6] Garber, Alan M., "Advances in cost-effectiveness analysis of health interventions," In: Culyer, A. J., Joseph P. Newhouse (Eds.), Handbook of Health Economics, vol. 1A. North-Holland, Amsterdam, 181-221 (2000).

[7] Garber, Alan M., and Mark J. Sculpher, "Cost Effectiveness and Payment Policy" In: Pauly, M.V., McGuire T. G. and Barros, P. P. (Eds.), Handbook of Health Economics, vol. 2. North-Holland, Amsterdam, 471-497 (2012).

[8] Garber, Alan M., and Charles E. Phelps, "Economic foundations of cost-effectiveness analysis," *Journal of Health Economics* 16, 1-31 (1997).

[9] Graff Zivin J., and Matthew Neidell, "The Impact of Pollution on Worker Productivity: Dataset," *American Economic Review*, 3652-3673 (2012).

[10] Graff Zivin J., and Matthew Neidell, "Environment, Health, and Human Capital," *Journal of Economic Literature* 51 (3), 689-730 (2013).

[11] Grossman, Michael, "On the concept of health capital and the demand for health," *Journal of Political Economy* 80, 223-55 (1972).

[12] Hall Robert E., and Charles I. Jones, "The Value of Life and the Rise in Health Spending," *The Quarterly Journal of Economics*, vol. 122, 39-72 (2007).

[13] Harrington Winston and Paul R. Portney, "Valuing the Benefits of Health and Safety Regulation," *Journal of Urban Economics* 22, 101-112 (1987).

[14] Meltzer, David, "Accounting for future costs in medical cost-effectiveness analysis," *Journal of Health Economics* 16 (1), 33-64 (1997).

[15] Meltzer, David, and Peter C. Smith, "Theoretical Issues Relevant to the Economic Evaluation of Health" In: Pauly, M.V., McGuire T. G. and Barros, P. P. (Eds.), Handbook of Health Economics, vol. 2. North-Holland, Amsterdam, 433-469 (2012).

[16] Murphy, Kevin M., and Topel, Robert H. (Eds.), "Measuring the Gains from Medical Research," *An Economic Research*, The University of Chicago Press, Chicago & London, 41-73 (2003).

[17] Neidell, Matthew J., "Air Pollution, Health, and Socio-Economic Status: The Effect of Outdoor Air Quality on Childhood Asthma," *Journal of Health Economics* 23 (6), 1209-36 (2004).

[18] Pauly, M.V., McGuire T. G. and Barros, P. P. (Eds.), Handbook of Health Economics, vol. 2. North-Holland, Amsterdam, (2012).

[19] Phelps, Charles E., *Health Economics*, Fourth ed., Pearson, Boston, (2010).

[20] Weinstein, Milton C., and Manning Jr. Willard G., "Theoretical issues in cost-effectiveness analysis," *Journal of Health Economics* 16 (1), 121-128 (1997).

Chapter 4

Measuring Global Flow of Funds: Theoretical Framework, Data Sources and Approaches

Nan Zhang
Faculty of Economic Sciences, Hiroshima Shudo University
1-1 Ozuka-Higashi 1-chome, Asaminami-ku, Hiroshima, 731-3195 Japan

Abstract

The main purpose of this paper is a trial to measure Global Flow of Funds (GFF), it includes four portions. Firstly, the paper will give a definition on GFF, based on the definition to decide the statistical domains of GFF, and build a statistical monitoring system for GFF using economic concepts and theoretical frameworks. Secondly, the paper sets out the concepts and existing data sources and integrates the data sources for measure GFF which are reflected in the Balance of Payments, International Investment Position (IIP), the Coordinated Direct Investment Survey (CDIS), the Coordinated Portfolio Investment Survey (CPIS), Consolidated Banking Statistics (CBS), and in the "rest-of-the-world" account of the national accounts. These datasets provide valuable information for the analysis of GFF. Thirdly, The Balance Sheet Approach is used to break down the rest of the world by components of IIP. An external statistics' matrix (metadata) exercise shows what external sector financial data are available by IIP concept. As the outcome of the study, this paper compiled Global Flow of Find Matrix with the pattern of "Country by Country" matrix. Fourthly, as well as an example illustrating how the GFF matrix operates.

Keywords:
Global Flow of Funds, Integrating Framework, IMF data, BIS data, Systemic Risk.

1. Introduction

In April 2009, the G-20 Finance Ministers and Central Bank Governors Working Group on Reinforcing International Co-operation and Promoting Integrity in Financial Markets called on the International Monetary Fund (IMF) and the Financial Stability Board (FSB) to explore information gaps and provide appropriate proposals for strengthening data collection and reporting back to the Finance Ministers and Central Bank Governors. As a result of the meeting, the IMF and FSB proposed maintenance and expansion of the resultant statistics in October 2009. The principal focus centered on Recommendation 15, as financial and economic crises are characterized by abrupt revaluations or other changes in the capital positions of key sectors of the economy. Recommendation 15 states that, "The IAG, which includes all agencies represented in the Inter-Secretariat Working Group on National Accounts, to develop a strategy to promote the compilation and dissemination of the Balance Sheet Approach (BSA), Flow of Funds, and sectoral data more generally, starting with the G-20 economies. Data on nonbank financial institutions should be a particular priority," etc.[1] Thus, Recommendation 15 also implies, through its reference to compiling "flow of funds" statistics, compilation of breakdowns of the financial positions and flows of each economic sector by its counterparty sectors. Datasets providing this kind of information are said to provide "from-whom-to-whom" financial statistics. In such a situation, we also need to understand and measure the flow of funds between countries, namely the Global Flow of Funds (GFF).

On the other hand, there is international awareness of the issue that the existing statistical data does not describe the risks inherent in a financial system. Previous research has evolved into discussion about the basic concept of GFF and a proposal to make a statistical framework for GFF. The recent global crisis showed how easily shocks in one country are transmitted and amplified, and rapid illiquidity in financial markets spread quickly across national borders. Therefore, IMF's Statistics Department has already organized seven economies with systemically important financial centers to construct a GFF mapping domestic and external capital stocks, geographically broken down, etc.[2] This means that the observation of GFF has not just remained in theoretical research, but has also entered the stage of experiment and statistical application. GFF is the extension of domestic flow of funds. It connects domestic economies with the rest of the world.[3] GFF data would provide valuable information for analyzing interconnectedness across borders, global liquidity flows, and global financial interdependencies.

This paper referenced "the report of the Financial Crisis and Information Gaps" that was prepared by the IMF and the FSB. The main purpose of the paper was to measure GFF and apply the result to regular monitoring of the GFF. The composition of this paper is as follows. Firstly, according to the concept of GFF, this paper will make an integrated framework for measuring GFF. Secondly, data sources and approach, is also very important. The paper sets out the concepts and existing data sources, and the BSA is used to break down the rest of the world by components of IMF data sources and BIS data sources. The third part, the paper discusses designing a GFF matrix through the use of metadata and base on the From-Whom-to-Whom framework. As the outcome of the study, the fourth part of this paper will give an example to explain the method for setting up GFF matrix with the pattern of "Country by Country". The main outcomes and the issues which remain are summarized within the conclusion.

2. An Integrated Framework for Global Flow of Funds

In order to measure financial stress and observe the spread effect of systematic financial crisis through GFF, that needs a new statistical framework which corresponds to the operational structure of GFF. Especially, an integrated framework should be used as the foundation of a statistical monitoring system. When the flow of funds in financial markets is tied up with the balance of payments, the rest of the world sector will have fund outflow excess (net capital outflows) if the current account is in surplus. Conversely, the domestic sector will have fund inflow excess. Therefore, when the real economic side of the domestic and overseas economy is analyzed under an open economic system, the balance of savings-investment of the domestic economy corresponds to the current account balance. However,

---

[1] Financial Stability Board and International Monetary Fund (2009). The Financial Crisis and Information aps Gaps-Report to the G-20 Finance Ministers and Central Bank Governors, p. 10.
[2] Luca Errico, et al.,(2013)
[3] Nan Zhang, (2005)

domestic net funds outflow corresponds with the capital account balance when we examine the financial relationship between domestic flow of funds and external flow of funds. For this reason, relationships among the domestic savings-investment balance, the financial surplus or deficit, the current account, and the external flow of funds should be expressed in an integrated framework to provide joint routine monitoring of GFF.

According to the definition of GFF, and in order to allow for the integration of Real and Financial Accounts for measuring GFF, we must set up an integrated framework for GFFS, as seen in Table 1.

Table 1. A Framework for Measuring Global Flow of Funds

Stocks	Flows	Stocks
Opening Balance Sheet	Transactions Other Changes	Closing Balance Sheet
Nonfinancial Assets	Savings-Investment Balance	Nonfinancial Assets
	Current Account Balance	
Assets (by financal category)		Assets (by financal category)
Direct Investment		Direct Investment
Portfolio Investment		Portfolio Investment
Other investment		Other investment
Reserves Assets		Reserves Assets
Total Assets	Change in Financial Assets	Total Assets
Liabilities (by financial category)		Liabilities (by financial category)
Direct Investment		Direct Investment
Portfolio Investment		Portfolio Investment
Other investment		Other investment
Total Liabilities	Change in Financial Liabilities	Total Liabilities
Net Position	Change in Net Worth	Net Position

The integrated framework is based on the BSA, using data from stocks. First, for integrating Real and Financial Accounts, we put items in the nonfinancial assets, savings-investment balance and current balance categories in a position in the flow diagram to show the structural relationship of real economies and financial economies in GFF. Within the financial category, we include financial assets, financial liabilities, and net position, as seen in Table 1. Four aspects of external financial positions and flows should be monitored: 1) an indication of any influence on current accounts from changes in economic structure which causes savings-investment imbalances; 2) an indication of any risks in international capital flow caused by a surplus or a deficit of domestic funds; 3) an indication of any shocks to international capital flow caused by an imbalance in current accounts, and by international large-scale capital inflows or outflows; 4) an indication of any causes of change in foreign exchange reserves and pressure of financial instability from rapid changes in foreign exchange reserves. Using the integrated framework to construct GFF would provide valuable information for the analysis of interconnectedness across borders, global liquidity flows, and global financial interdependencies. And the framework could also be extended to flow data. For this next step, we would then break down the data sources by sector and counterpart country.

3. The Data Sources for Global Flow of Funds

The metadata of GFFS should be based on existing statistical data, and therefore have many similarities of approach with them. The data sources for GFF include not only the "rest-of-the-world" account of national accounts, but also balance of payment, monetary and financial statistics, IIP statistics and BIS international banking statistics. Two metadata matrices are then discussed, which summarize the concepts, draw out what data are available, and identify the major data gaps. These two matrices cover the Domestic Assets and Liabilities (DAL) and the External Assets and Liabilities (EAL). The matrix could be extended to flow data.

The DAL matrix is based on the Balance Sheet Approach (BSA), with the rest of the world sector data drawn from the National Accounts and IIP. The EAL matrix presents metadata on whatever external sector financial stock data are available, by IIP category, drawing on IMF and BIS data sources. The IIP is the link between the domestic and external matrices.

Data from IMF's Monetary and Financial Statistics, IIP and the National Accounts are used to derive the BSA matrix. The BSA matrix can provide information about a country or region's financial corporations' stock positions for residents and nonresidents. In the EAL matrix, the datasets with bilateral counterpart country details collected by the IMF and BIS are as follows.

(i) Foreign direct investment[4]: The Coordinated Direct Investment Survey (CDIS) provides bilateral counterpart country details on "inward" direct investment positions (i.e., direct investment into the reporting economy) cross-classified by economy of immediate investor, and data on "outward" direct investment positions (i.e., direct investment abroad by the reporting economy), cross-classified by economy of immediate investment, as well as mirror data for all economies.

(ii) Portfolio investment: The Coordinated Portfolio Investment Survey (CPIS) provides bilateral counterpart country details covering holdings of asset stock positions by reporting economies and derived (mirror[5]) liabilities for all economies. The purpose of the CPIS is to improve statistics of holdings of portfolio investment assets in the form of equity, long-term debt, and short-term debt. It is also used to collect comprehensive information, with geographical detail on the country of residence of the issuer, on the stock of cross-border equities, long-term bonds and notes, and on short-term debt instruments for use in the compilation or improvement of IIP statistics on portfolio investment capital.

(iii) Other investment: Other investment is a residual category that includes positions and transactions other than those included in direct investment, portfolio investment, financial derivatives and employee stock options, and reserve assets.[6] Other investment includes: (a) other equity; (b) currency and deposits; (c) loans (including use of IMF credit and loans from the IMF); (d) nonlife insurance technical reserves, life insurance and annuities entitlements, pension entitlements, and provisions for calls under standardized guarantees; (e) trade credit and advances; (f) other accounts receivable/payable; and (g) SDR allocations (SDR holdings are included in reserve assets). In order to reflect the bilateral counterpart country for loans, deposits, and other assets and liabilities, this paper put the related dataset with BIS International Banking Statistics (IBS) instead of IIP Statistics.

(iv) The BIS compiles and publishes two sets of statistics on international banking activity, which includes Locational Banking Statistics (LBS) and Consolidated Banking Statistics (CBS). This paper utilizes LBS in the dataset, because the BIS locational data provides quarterly information on claims and liabilities of banks vis-à-vis banks and nonbanks located in other countries worldwide. They are based on the economy of location or residence of the creditor bank and can also be used to mirror data for non-reporting countries. They are used in the external statistics' matrix.

(v) For data on reserve assets: The Data Template for the Balance of Payment, the IIP and Currency Composition of Official Foreign Exchange Reserves (COFER) provide country-level data, while the

---

[4] See Luca Errico et al., 2013.
[5] Mirror data refers to the same data as seen from different perspectives. For instance, banks' loans to households could be said to be mirror data of household debt to banks.
[6] IMF, *Balance of Payments Manual,* 6th edition (BPM6), 111.

Survey of Securities Held as Foreign Exchange Reserves (SEFER) provides counterpart country data for all SEFER reporters as a group.[7] For supplementing data on reserve assets, International Financial Statistics (IFS) which includes World Total Reserves, World Gold, World Reserve Position in the Fund, World SDR Holdings and World Foreign Exchange, can also be used.

In this paper, IIP data have been used to supplement the data for constructing the EAL matrix. The IIP is a subset of the national balance sheet, the net IIP plus the value of nonfinancial assets equaling the net worth of the economy, which is the balancing item of the national balance sheet. The IIP relates to a point in time, usually at the beginning of the period (opening value) or the end of the period (closing value).

GFFS can construct a statistical framework if concepts, definitions and classifications underlying these statistics are standardized across economies. Fortunately, we can get these standards from *2008SNA*, the IMF's *Monetary and Financial Statistics Manual 2000*, *Balance of Payments Manual (BPM6)*, and the BIS's *Guidelines for Reporting the BIS International Banking Statistics*.

4. Global Flow of Funds Matrix on a From-Whom-to-Whom Basis

As a transitional preparation for making the EAL matrix, we made the DAL matrix (Table 2) first. Table 2 shows for the rest of the world sector each financial instrument: stocks of the issuer of a liability (the debtor) on the horizontal axis, and stocks of the holder of a liability (the creditor) on the vertical axis. The DAL matrix is based on the BSA matrix methodology. The matrix identifies five sectors, the data for the rest of the world and how it relates to: (i) general government; (ii) financial corporations; (iii) nonfinancial corporations; and (iv) the household sector. Each column corresponds to the balance sheet of the sector in question, and the assets and liabilities are then listed in the rows by instrument, with the counterparty sectors identified for each cell.

Table 2. Domestic Assets and Liabilities Matrix by Balance Sheet Approach

Issuer of liability (debtor) / Holder of liability (creditor)	General Government			Financial Sector			Nonfinancial Corporations			Household			Rest of the World		
	A	L	NP	A	L	NP	A	L	NP	A	L	NP	A	L	NP
Nonresidents															
Currency and deposits															
Securities other than shares															
Loans															
Shares and other equity															
Insurance technical reserves															
Financial derivatives															
Other accounts receivable															

The rest of the world sector data are drawn from the IIP; assets in the IIP are recorded as liabilities of nonresidents in the BSA, and IIP liabilities represent nonresidents' claims in the BSA. Cross-border liabilities of debtors are along the horizontal axis, and cross-border claims of asset holders along the vertical axis, for each financial instrument.

The *SNA* provides an integrated framework for developing financial positions and flows on a from-whom-to-whom basis because its underlying principles ensure that the linkages of the economic and

---

[7] Luca Errico et al., 2013.

financial actions of an economy are captured. However, the *SNA* standard presentation is not explicitly designed to show the inter-sectoral linkages, as traditionally it has focused primarily on answering "who does what," but not "who does what with whom." Therefore, in the case of the DAL, we must also include "from-whom-to-whom" information on the matrix (See Table 3).

Table 3. Domestic Assets and Liabilities Matrix on a From-Whom-to-Whom Basis

Issuer of liability (debtor) / Holder of liability (creditor)	Residents				Nonresidents	All Debtors
	General Government	Financial Sector	Nonfinancial Corporations	Household		
Residents — General Government						
Residents — Financial Sector						
Residents — Nonfinancial Corporations						
Residents — Household						
Nonresidents						
All Creditors						

Table 3 shows the integrated framework of the DAL on a from-whom-to-whom basis by institutional sector, and the rest of the world in a matrix format. For an economy, it shows transactions, revaluations, other changes in the volume of assets and liabilities, and positions for a financial instrument acquired/held by residents (grouped into (sub) sectors) and nonresidents vis-à-vis institutional units as debtors, broken down by residency and by institutional sector (cells of Table 3 shaded grey).

The objective of the GFF approach employed in this paper is to produce full domestic and EAL matrices. Once we have these, we can link the rest of the world sector with EAL to construct the EAL matrix through the DAL matrix. The EAL matrix is also based on the BSA (see Table 4), that depicts for the rest of the world sector, the main countries for observation and Other Economies with each financial instrument/ stock of the issuer of a liability (the debtor) on the horizontal axis, and stocks of the holder of a liability (the creditor) on the vertical axis. It is the external flow of funds matrix for the observed countries or regions, where the external assets and liabilities have been disaggregated into the counterpart country, by instrument.

Table 4. External Assets and Liabilities Matrix

Issuer of liability (debtor) / Holder of liability (creditor)	Rest of the World			Country A			Country B ···			Other Economies		
	A	L	NP	A	L	NP	A	L	NP	A	L	NP
Direct Investment												
Portfolio Investment												
Equity Securities												
Debt Securities												
Long-time debt securities												
Short-time debt securities												
Other Investment Banks												
Non-banks												
Reserve Position in the Fund												
SDR Holdings												
Foreign Exchange												
Total IIP												

Table 4 provides a statistical framework for presenting cross-border stocks, by counterpart country and sector and instrument. It shows available external sector financial assets and liabilities' stock data broken down by country, sector of investor, and investee. Columns 2-4 of the EAL matrix are taken from the last three columns of Table 2. The matrix presents external financial asset and liability positions, showing available data by IIP category and instrument: direct investment, portfolio investment equity and debt securities (the latter displayed separately for long-term and short-term debt), other investment (separately for banks and others, using the BIS international banking statistics), and reserve assets. Table 4 shows what may be possible in a GFF framework for a country which enables the monitoring of financial positions, both regional/national and cross-border (by country and by sector).

Although Table 4 is modeled after a traditional account form, it cannot show the intersectoral from-whom-to-whom relationships needed to measure financial positions and flows. As the *SNA* is the internationally accepted methodology for the compilation of national accounts, the lack of prominence it gives to the from-whom-to whom principle for data compilation and presentation may be one of the reasons why these statistics are not more widely used. Therefore, in order to know "who is financing whom, in what amount, and with which type of financial instrument," we constructed the EAL matrix on a from-whom-to-whom basis. The following proposed Table 5 reflects this approach and shows the financial instrument categories according to *2008SNA*.

Table 5. External Assets and Liabilities Matrix on a From-Whom-to-Whom Basis

Counterpart Countries (Investment in):	Counterpart Countries (Investment from):				
	Rest of the World	Country A	Country B	. . .	Other Economies
Rest of the World					
Country A					
Country B					
. . .					
Other Economies					

According to analytical need, the EAL matrix resulting from the from-whom-to-whom table can be created to illustrate "Country vis-à-vis Country" through each financial instrument. These instruments show the connections between financial transactions, such as "direct investment," "portfolio investment," etc. Likewise, every financial instrument can disaggregate within the matrix on a from-whom-to-whom basis. Instruments located in the "rows" of the table describe a country relative to the counterpart country's assets, while instruments located in the "columns" describe a country relative to the counterpart country's liabilities. If all the financial instruments are totaled, that amount will equal the sum total of external financial assets and liabilities in the given country. In this way, external assets and liabilities will have been disaggregated into the counterpart country, and by main instruments.

The from-whom-to-whom compilation approach also enhances the quality and consistency of data by providing more cross-checking and balancing opportunities. When the information in Table 4 is combined with that in Table 5, we can map out the complete bilateral relationship between national/regional economies using stock data. The matrices could potentially be extended to flow data to quantify gross bilateral flows into: (i) transactions; (ii) changes in the value of a financial asset/liability; and (iii) other changes in the volume of an asset/liability. Using Table 5 we can answer the compound question, "Who is financing whom, in what amount, and with which type of financial instrument?" In the next section we will give an example to explain the method for setting up GFF matrix with the pattern of

"Country by Country".

5. An Example for Setting up a Global Flow of Funds Matrix

Based on the layout of Table 4, the objective of the GFF outlined in this paper is to produce external stock matrices. As an example, we compiled Table 6. Table 6 shows what may be possible in a GFF framework for pivotal countries which would enable the monitoring of financial positions both by region/nation and cross-border (by country and instrument).

Table 6 is an illustration of the BSA matrix for External Assets and Liabilities at the end of 2012. The rows of the matrix depict Direct Investment (DI), Portfolio Investment (PI), Other Investment Banks (OI) and Reserve Assets (RA), covering the main structural elements of external financial stocks. The assets and liabilities are then listed by instrument in the rows, with the counterparty sectors identified for each cell. The columns of the matrix identify twelve sectors: ten country sectors, all other economies, and a world sector. The total of each sector's assets or liabilities is equal to the world's assets or liabilities. The columns of the matrix are set up to show the external assets or liabilities situation for many countries, thereby displaying both national and regional perspectives. Each column corresponds to the balance sheet of the sector in question; which countries or regions should appear in the matrix depends on the specific purpose of the analysis.

Table 6. BSA Matrix for External Assets and Liabilities

(End-of-Period, US Dollars, Millions, December 2012)

	Canada		China		France		Germany		Japan		Luxembourg	
	A	L	A	L	A	L	A	L	A	L	A	L
Direct Investment	533759	629825	552044	2068027	1233748	1029813	1152733	1001498	1054099	222153	2125939	2440342
Portfolio Investment	891583	1253212	5619	643260	2570100	2876813	2760141	3061649	3525267	2085547	3056548	2321408
Equity Securities	690635	494591	25	504325	637798	756407	747415	742815	687170	965403	1202086	1664445
Debt Securities	200948	761539	5595	138936	1932302	2120404	2012726	2334977	2838097	1120144	1854462	656963
Long-time debt securities	197872	660731	5595	55739	1664702	1858452	1978472	2131190	2811498	39808	1552510	604806
Short-time bebt securities	3076	88606	0	82559	267601	262983	34254	203899	26599	284646	301952	47135
Other Investment Banks	485956	346953	1052748	942553	2363167	2175738	2455972	1231831	1766504	1871218	763241	552795
Non-banks	211349	87170	45663	38399	890872	444387	962319	311425	65901	18881	251759	159957
Reserve Assets	68529		3387863		205093		248857		1264796		991	
Monetary Gold	181		56743		152404		181435		40829		120	
Special Drawing Rights	8754		11356		14586		17908		19910		375	
Reserve Position in the Fund	4368		8175		8474		11549		13659		345	
Other Reserve Assets	55226		3311589		29630		37964		1190398		151	
Total IIP	1979827	2229990	4998274	3653841	6372108	6082363	6617703	5294978	7610664	4178918	5946719	5314545
Net IIP	-250163		1344433		289745		1322726		3431746		632174	

Data Source: Coordinated Direct Investment Survey (CDIS), Coordinated Portfolio Investment Survey (CPIS), International Financial Statistics (IFS) and IIP data extracted from IMF Data Warehouse http://www.imf.org/external/data.htm on 6/17/2015; BIS international banking statistics, http://www.bis.org/statistics/consstats.htm on 1/20/2015.

Notes:
(i) Since there aren't the data of China's other investment banks in BIS statistics, this paper used other investment statistics of IIP instead of BIS data.

(ii) The Other Investment Banks total may not balance, because its statistical scope doesn't include the entire world.
(iii) (-) Relevant data are not included in IMF Data; "0" indicates a value less than US$ 500,000.

Table 6. BSA Matrix for External Assets and Liabilities (Continued)

	Netherlands		Switzerland		United Kingdom		United States		All Other Economies		World	
	A	L	A	L	A	L	A	L	A	L	A	L
Direct Investment	1031308	664716	1064577	732654	2396519	1271425	3198178	2650832	11990653	13622271	26333556	26333556
Portfolio Investment	1555383	1641674	1183494	713966	3551807	3689233	7917764	9007214	16563223	16286953	43580927	43580927
Equity Securities	683968	466655	486972	621288	1220533	1687119	5311506	2731964	5285737	6318831	16953844	16953844
Debt Securities	871415	1158292	696521	92678	2331274	2002373	2606258	6274794	11277486	9965984	26627084	26627084
Long-time debt securities	172564	941461	629617	70474	2201982	1719543	2241201	5633505	10287815	10028119	23743827	23743827
Short-time bebt securities	36737	148493	66905	43	129292	282642	365057	641145	1653222	842545	2884696	2884696
Other Investment Banks	1032701	980406	684742	797782	5376628	4785132	3186054	3529782	10043780	7873863	29211492	25088053
Non-banks	0	972958	188510	478287	2428243	1676321	985595	1092761	5567995	2349947	11598206	7630493
Reserve Assets	54816		529161		97958		572368		1026837		7457271	
Monetary Gold	32766		55391		16113		433434		-		-	
Special Drawing Rights	7163		4654		14786		55050		49634		204177	
Reserve Position in the Fund	4084		3071		8863		34161		6496		103244	
Other Reserve Assets	10803		466045		58197		49723		-		-	
Total IIP	3674208	3286797	3461974	2244402	11422912	9745789	14874364	15187828	39624493	37783086	99125975	95002536
Net IIP	387411		1217572		1677123		-313464		1841407		4123439	

The data in Table 6 is derived from IMF Data Warehouse and BIS International Banking Statistics. More specifically, the Direct Investment section used CDIS data, the Portfolio Investment section used CPIS data, the Other Investment Banks section used BIS locational banking statistics, and the Reserve Assets section used IIP data. Through actual data validation, we found that building an integrated data source framework is an effective method for measuring GFF. Using this method, the four sections mentioned about *(DI+PI+OI+RA)* are added back in to the calculation to avoid double counting or under-recording. However, even if each country in the same report submits its data to IMF or BIS, data submission details between countries differ when reporting the same indicator. For example, China has not yet submitted Other Investment Banks data to the BIS, so data in the report which draw upon the BIS as a data source are missing. In this particular case, we chose the same indicators within IIP data instead of BIS data, and used this data to populate the related cells in Table 7. In addition, total reserve assets data are not included in IIP data; we therefore used international financial statistics instead of IIP data for this item. Unfortunately, data gaps will continue to present a problem in the measurement of GFF.

Based on the layout of Table 5, we set up Table 7 and Table 8 on a country by country basis. This kind of matrix can not only show bilateral stocks by financial instrument, but also illustrate the exact situation of each instrument according to its use and source among main countries. That is, it can indicate the EAL on a from-whom-to-whom basis. As an actual example, limited to the information in the collected data source, we used the CDIS data and the CPIS data (both issued by IMF data) to compile the EAL matrices.

Table 7 contains EAL matrices at the ten countries for the end of 2012, where the external assets and liabilities have been disaggregated into counterpart countries, and likewise by direct investment item. Just as Table 7 is derived from the first row of Table 6, it is also a detailed description of the data in Table 6. This qualification method is based on the ratio of direct investment in the global market and trading counterpart economies. Considering the direct investment of bilateral relations, we selected data associated with ten countries, namely Canada, China, France, Germany, Japan, Luxembourg, the Netherlands, Switzerland, the United Kingdom and the United States, to compile the DI matrix. Cross-border liabilities of debtors appear along the horizontal axis, and cross-border claims of asset holders along the vertical axis, for each financial instrument.

Using Table 7, we can both determine the distribution and scale of direct investment, and show the basic structure of direct investment. By analyzing the rows of the matrix, we can know where direct investment in a country originates from, and through an analysis of the columns of the matrix we can see where a country's own direct investment takes place. At the same time, we also know that the total of the rows in the matrix will always equal the total of the columns.

Moreover, based on the structure of Table 5, we compiled Table 8 for mapping portfolio investment. The PI matrix fully corresponds to the second row of the BSA matrix, and provides a conceptual framework for presenting cross-border positions by counterpart country and by instrument. We used CPIS data to build Table 8, but chose to use Hong Kong's data instead of China's data as China's data isn't included in CPIS data. The structure and usage of Table 8 are basically the same as Table 7.

When the information in Table 6 is combined with that in Table 7 and Table 8, we can map out complete bilateral relationships between national/regional economies using CDIS, CPIS, BIS and IIP data. The matrices could potentially be extended to flow data to quantify gross bilateral flows into: (i) transactions; (ii) changes in the value of a financial asset/liability; and (iii) other changes in the volume of an asset/liability.

6. Concluding Remarks

This paper reviewed the definition of GFF, clarified the integrated framework for measuring GFF, and attempted to carry out the compilation of the GFFS for external financial positions and flows on a from-whom-to-whom basis. In addition, it will potentially fill some important data gaps in currently available macroeconomic statistics. The paper elaborates on the main attributes of the integrated macroeconomic accounts and the GFF matrix, which allows it to serve as the framework for compiling sector accounts, including financial positions and flows on a from-whom-to-whom basis. In particular, the GFF integrated framework ensures three consistency rules as follows:

The core statistical structure of the GFFS for external financial positions and flows focuses on showing not only who does what, but also includes who does what with whom. This paper recommends that the GFFS becomes a part of the SNA in the future to incorporate the from-whom-to-whom relationship as the main underlying principle for compiling and disseminating external financial positions and flows.

The advantage of using IMF and BIS data to compile a GFF matrix within the integrated SNA framework (as opposed to using fragmentary data from different sources) is that such a framework ensures data consistency for all entities and for all economic flows and positions, and thus allows for a systematic understanding of the relationships between economic flows in the real and the financial spheres; financial interconnectedness; and linkages between the domestic economic and external economic matrices (e.g., between savings-investment, financial surplus or deficit, or balance of payment and international capital flows).

Table 7. Inward Direct Investment Positions by pivotal Reporting Economies Cross-classified by Counterpart Economies

(As of end-2012, US Dollars, Millions)

Counterpart Economy (Investment from):	Canada	China, P.R.: Mainland	France	Germany	Japan	Luxembourg	Netherlands	Switzerland	United Kingdom	United States	All Other Economies	Total Investment
Canada	-	8045	12765	3184	1767	88059	22592	454	31865	225331	139696	533759
China, P.R.: Mainland	16524	-	619	2012	550	20612	2666	c	3224	5154	500683	552044
France	9525	16587	-	86884	17985	69958	145710	42351	107634	209121	527992	1233748
Germany	9239	39464	98977	-	8364	74931	163273	32356	84093	199006	443028	1152733
Japan	16331	129388	15481	21912	-	2589	73439	3616	51713	308253	385456	1008178
Luxembourg	27885	3914	135968	148593	2943	-	561597	146499	77986	202338	818216	2125939
Netherlands	67303	21917	170197	243107	31524	252007	-	180207	197659	274904	1442836	2881660
Switzerland	18389	10852	78411	86616	13473	103892	203550	-	64214	203954	281226	1064577
United Kingdom	48913	18795	115484	84296	15430	499790	457434	13308	-	486833	656237	2396519
United States	321660	62960	101488	99371	61592	375351	791171	94702	331296	-	958586	3198178
All Other Economies	94055	1756104	300422	225523	52124	953152	1326551	219160	321742	535938	-	10186221
Total Investment	629825	2068027	1029813	1001498	205752	2440342	3747982	732654	1271425	2650832	10555405	26333556

Data Source: Coordinated Direct Investment Survey (CDIS), Data extracted from IMF Data Warehouse on 6/13/2015

http://data.imf.org/?sk=40313609-F037-48C1-84B1-E1F1CE54D6D5&ss=1393552803658

Notes: (i) Direct investment positions are negative when a direct investor's claims (equity and/or debt) on its direct investment enterprise are less than the direct investment enterprise's claims (equity and/or debt) on its direct investor.

(ii) Direct investment positions also can be negative due to negative retained earnings (which may result from the accumulation of negative reinvested earnings).

(iii) Blank cells reflect data not available or not applicable and cells with "c" reflect data that were suppressed by the reporting economy to preserve confidentiality.

(iv) Totals may not be equal to the sum of their components due to rounding.

Table 8. Geographic Breakdown of pivotal Portfolio Investment: Total Portfolio Investment

(Derived from Creditor Data, as of end 2012, US Dollars, Millions)

Investment from: / Investment in:	Canada	China, P.R.: Hong Kong	France	Germany	Japan	Luxembourg	Netherlands	Switzerland	United Kingdom	United States	All Other Economies	Total Investment
Canada	...	8,658	19,383	20,238	61,176	43,173	16,370	29,729	26,918	808,022	219,544	1,253,212
China, P.R.: Hong Kong	10,498	-	6,999	3,467	16,984	34,988	10,827	4,173	41,559	144,743	87,740	361,979
France	27,667	10,328	...	375,394	215,947	287,615	185,484	97,155	234,528	369,813	1,072,882	2,876,813
Germany	20,647	13,118	255,107	-	181,490	338,000	266,771	89,938	301,460	325,218	1,269,900	3,061,649
Japan	37,099	37,295	108,138	23,173	-	62,636	34,041	20,085	183,940	506,339	413,402	1,426,147
Luxembourg	5,996	39,326	203,882	455,628	91,552	-	89,631	162,863	103,492	104,733	1,064,304	2,321,408
Netherlands	11,669	9,054	319,363	266,528	127,933	152,038	-	79,534	220,192	286,054	526,100	1,998,465
Swizerland	17,356	1,973	24,547	35,831	24,199	45,582	28,913	-	71,248	333,492	130,824	713,966
United Kingdom	69,956	69,285	230,967	222,051	215,929	224,784	122,787	73017	-	1,128,508	1,331,950	3,689,233
United States	516,425	78,344	201,672	219,577	1,183,093	606,112	350,707	177,216	848,455	-	4,825,612	9,007,214
All Other Economies	174,269	719,844	1,200,042	1,138,253	1,406,963	1,261,620	552,434	449,782	1,520,014	3,910,842		16,870,844
Total Investment	891,583	987,223	2,570,100	2,760,141	3,525,267	3,056,548	1,657,965	1,183,494	3,551,807	7,917,764	15,479,037	43,580,927

Data Source: Coordinated Portfolio Investment Survey (CPIS), Data extracted from IMF Data Warehouse on 6/11/2015 5:42:16 PM

http://data.imf.org/?sk=B981B4E3-4E58-467E-9B90-9DE0C3367363

Notes: "0" Indicates a value less than US$ 500,000, "c" Indicates data are confidential, (-) Indicates that a figure is zero,

Finally, according to the statistical framework, this paper gave an example, clarified the GFF matrices methodology, and outlined the specific source of data. This paper suggests that, considering the difficulties that countries are likely to face in compiling GFF accounts, implementation could occur in steps depending on current statistical development status, resource requirements, and analytical and policy needs. As GFF statistics are established and perfected in the future, the following steps should also be taken:

(i). In order to establish GFF statistics, there is a need to integrate data sources that include CDIS, CPIS, IIP, IFS and BIS statistics, etc. in accordance with the creation standard of the *SNA*. There is likewise a need to set up the GFF account to connect with the Flow of Funds account in the *SNA*. This, however, requires additional external financial positions in new data collection systems, as described above for GFFS databases.

(ii). For the rest of the world by main sector, further details for the main observation countries by subsectors and other economic flows may also be considered. From-whom-to-whom external financial positions, flows for subsectors of the main observation countries, and possibly other economic flows should be taken into account.

(iii). Sectors (subsectors) and specific instruments (loans, deposits, direct investment, portfolio investment, other investment banks, reserve position in the Fund, and foreign exchange) of financial positions and flows on a from-whom-to-whom basis should ideally move from aggregated subsector and instrument details towards disaggregated subsector and instrument details.

(iv). Lastly, the BSA and external matrices could potentially be extended to flow data to identify transactions, revaluation changes, and other changes in volume of an asset/liability. This may be an even more challenging task, given that the flow data would need to be broken down by counterpart country, as relevant.

Acknowledgements

I have completed this research at Stanford University as a visiting scholar from September 2014 until August 2015. The department of Statistics at Stanford University provided me with a very good study environment. I more would like to thank Professor Tze Leung Lai for supporting my work. I had a lot of inspiration and product when I participated in his research team, seminar, workshop and lectures, and also enjoyed the campus of Stanford University. This paper is based on my presentation at IARIW-OECD conference.[8] I would also like to thank Mr. Dennis Fixler, Chief Statistician, Bureau of Economic Analysis at U.S. Department of Commerce, for his valuable comments on my paper.

References

[1] Bank for International Settlements, *Guidelines for reporting the BIS international banking statistics*, 2013.

---

[8] 2015 IARIW-OECD Conference: W(h)ither the SNA? April 16-17, 2015

[2] —, http://www.bis.org/statistics/consstats.htm
[3] Established Principal Global Indicators (PGI) Website: http://www.principalglobalindicators.org/default.aspx
[4] European Communities, International Monetary Fund, Organisation for Economic Co-operation and Development, United Nations and World Bank, *System of National Account 2008,* Sales No. E.08.XVII.29, United Nations, New York, 2009.
[5] Financial Stability Board and International Monetary Fund(2009) "The Financial Crisis and Information Gaps," Report to the G‐20 Finance Ministers and Central Bank Governors.
[6] IMF, *Balance of payments and international investment position manual*, 6th Edition (BPM6) (2009)
[7] —, *Financial Soundness Indicators Compilation Guide*, March 2006
[8] —, *Update of the Monetary and Financial Statistics Manual (MFSM) and the Monetary and Financial Statistics Compilation Guide (MFSCG)*
[9] —, http://www.imf.org/external/data.htm
[10] —, http://data.imf.org/?sk=40313609-F037-48C1-84B1-E1F1CE54D6D5&ss=1393552803658
[11] —, http://data.imf.org/?sk=B981B4E3-4E58-467E-9B90-9DE0C3367363
[12] Luca Errico, Artak Harutyunyan, Elena Loukoianova, Richard Walton, Yevgeniya Korniyenko, Goran Amidžić, Hanan AbuShanab, Hyun Song Shin, "Mapping the Shadow Banking System Through a Global Flow of Funds Analysis," IMF Working Paper WP/14/10, 2014.
[13] Luca Errico, Richard Walton, Alicia Hierro, Hanan AbuShanab, Goran Amidzic, "Global Flow of Funds: Mapping Bilateral Geographic Flows," Proceedings 59th ISI World Statistics Congress, 2825-2830, 2013.
[14] Manik Shrestha, Reimund Mink, and Segismundo Fassler, "An Integrated Framework for Financial Positions and Flows on a From-Whom-to-Whom Basis: Concepts, Status, and Prospects," IMF Working Paper WP/12/57, 2012.
[15] Nan Zhang, "New Frameworks for Measuring Global-Flow-of-Funds: Financial Stability in China", in the 32nd General Conference of The International Association for Research in Income and Wealth (IARIW), 2012.
[16] —, Measuring Global Flow of Funds and Integrating Real and Financial Accounts, Working paper, 2015 IARIW-OECD Conference: W(h)ither the SNA? April 16-17, 2015.
[17] Sadao Ishida, *Flow of Funds in Japanese Economy*, Toyo Keizai Shimpo-Sha, 170-205, 1993.
[18] Shrestha, Manik, Reimund Mink and Segismundo Fassler, "An Integrated Framework for Financial Positions and Flows on a From-Whom-to-Whom Basis: Concepts, Status, and Prospects," IMF Working Paper WP/12/57, 2012.

Chapter 5

A Comparative Study on Detecting Ridge Structure for Population-Based Optimization Algorithms

Setsuko Sakai and Tetsuyuki Takahama**
*Faculty of Commercial Sciences, Hiroshima Shudo University
1-1 Ozuka-Higashi 1-chome, Asaminami-ku, Hiroshima, JAPAN 731-3195
**Graduate School of Information Sciences, Hiroshima City University
4-1 Ozuka-Higashi 3-chome, Asaminami-ku, Hiroshima, JAPAN 731-3194*

Abstract

There exist many studies on solving optimization problems using population-based optimization algorithms (POAs). POAs such as evolutionary algorithms have been proved to be powerful function optimization algorithms and outperform conventional optimization algorithms. However, there exist some difficult optimization problems such as problems with ridge structure. In problems with ridge structure, search points will move through a narrow path to find better points, the diversity of search points will be lost, and the search process will be slowed down or even be stopped at a local solution. If ridge structure can be detected, the efficiency and robustness of the search process can be improved by selecting proper algorithm parameters to keep the diversity. In this study, we propose three methods of detecting ridge structure and also propose a method of controlling algorithm parameters adaptively for ridge structure. The performances of the methods are compared by optimizing several functions with controlling algorithm parameters.

Key Words:
Ridge structure, Population-based optimization algorithms, Evolutionary algorithms, Differential evolution

1. Introduction

There exist many studies on solving optimization problems using population-based optimization algorithms (POAs) in which a population or multiple search points are used to search for an optimal solution. In general, POAs are stochastic direct search methods, which only need function values to be optimized, and are easy to implement. For this reason, POAs have been successfully applied to various fields including science and engineering. Evolutionary algorithms (EAs) are population-based stochastic optimization algorithms which are inspired by biological evolution and include Genetic Algorithm (GA), Evolution Strategy (ES), Differential Evolution (DE) [1, 2] and so on. EAs have been proved to be powerful function optimization algorithms and outperform conventional optimization algorithms for various problems including discontinuous, non-differential, multimodal, noisy problems, and multi-objective problems.

In general, a disadvantage of evolutionary algorithms is that they need a large number of function evaluations before a well acceptable solution can be found. Recently, the size of optimization problems tends to become larger, and the cost of function evaluations becomes higher. It is necessary to develop more efficient optimization algorithms to reduce the number of function evaluations. Especially, problems with ridge structure are very difficult to solve efficiently. In the problems, search points will move through a narrow path to find better points, the diversity of search points will be lost, and the search process will be slowed down or even be stopped at a local solution.

In this study, we propose the following methods for detecting the ridge structure:

(1) When search points move through a narrow path, the best point often locates at a front position in search points. The distance between the best point and the other points will be large compared with the distance between a non-best point and the other points. Thus, some distance metric of the best point compared with the other points can be used to detect the ridge structure.

(2) When search points are distributed around a narrow path, the correlation among variables becomes large. Thus, some correlation metric can be used to detect the ridge structure.

If the ridge structure can be detected, algorithm parameters can be adjusted to keep the diversity of search points. The performance of the methods for detecting ridge structure is compared by optimizing several benchmark functions with adjusting algorithm parameters based on the proposed metrics. Differential evolution (DE) is adopted as a POA in this study.

In Section 2, related works are described. Three methods for detecting ridge structure are proposed in Section 3. In Section 4, DE is briefly explained and DE with detecting ridge structure is defined. The experimental results are shown in Section 5. Finally, conclusions are described in Section 6.

2. Related Works

Ridge structure is a typical landscape in optimization problems. Some studies on detecting landscape such as unimodal landscape and multimodal landscape have been done. In order to detect unimodal or multimodal landscape, it needs to decide the number of valleys because one valley exists in unimodal landscape and plural valleys exist in multimodal landscape. A valley point is the point of which function value is less than the function values of neighborhood points. The neighborhood relations among search points can be defined by using a self-organizing map, sampling, and a proximity graph [3]:

(a) Self-organizing map (SOM): A two-dimensional self-organizing map is created from search points. If the function value of a node is less than the function values of the neighbor nodes on the map, it is thought that the node corresponds to a valley in the function [4]. However, since higher dimensional search points are projected onto two-dimensional space, it is difficult to obtain correct neighborhood relations.

(b) Sampling: In this method, points which have apparent neighborhood relations are sampled. The method of sampling along a line is proposed [5–7]. However, extra function evaluations are needed to obtain objective values of sampled points. Also, landscape as a whole cannot be detected but landscape near the sampled points can be detected.

(c) Proximity graph: A proximity graph is created from search points. If two points are connected by an edge in the graph, the points have the neighborhood relation [8,9]. The number of valleys/hills can be estimated using the relation.

If landscape modality can be estimated, the algorithm parameters can be controlled properly. For example, if the landscape of the objective function is unimodal, the efficiency of the POAs can be improved by selecting parameters for local search around a best solution. If the landscape is multimodal, the robustness of the POAs can be improved by selecting parameters for global search in search space. However, any study on detecting ridge structure has not been done. In this study, three methods for detecting ridge structure are proposed and algorithm parameters are controlled to keep diversity of search points.

In order to improve the efficiency, many researchers have been studying on controlling the parameters and the strategies in EAs. The methods of the control can be classified into some categories. For example, following methods are proposed in DE [5].

(1) selection-based control: Strategies and parameter values are selected regardless of current search state. CoDE(composite DE) [10] generates three trial vectors using three strategies with randomly selected parameter values from parameter candidate sets and the best trial vector will head to the survivor selection.

(2) observation-based control: The current search state is observed, proper parameter values are inferred according to the observation, and parameters and/or strategies are dynamically controlled. FADE(Fuzzy Adaptive DE) [11] observes the movement of search points and the change of function values between successive generations, and controls F and CR. DESFC(DE with Speciation and Fuzzy Clustering) [12] adopts fuzzy clustering, observes partition entropy of search points, and controls CR and the mutation strategies between the rand and the species-best strategy.

(3) success-based control: It is recognized as a success case when a better search point than the parent is generated. The parameters and/or strategies are adjusted so that the values in the success cases are frequently used. It is thought that the self-adaptation, where parameters are contained in individuals and are evolved by applying evolutionary operators to the parameters, is included in this category. DESAP(Differential Evolution with Self-Adapting Populations) [13] controls F, CR and N self-adaptively. SaDE(Self-adaptive DE) [14] controls the selection probability of the mutation strategies according to the success rates and controls the mean value of CR for each strategy according to the mean value in success case. jDE(self-adaptive DE algorithm) [15] controls F and CR self-adaptively. JADE(adaptive DE with optional external archive) [16] and MDE_pBX(modified DE with p-best crossover) [17] control the mean and power mean values of F and CR according to the mean values in success cases.

In the category (1), useful knowledge to improve the search efficiency is ignored. In the category (2), it is difficult to select proper type of observation which is independent of the optimization problem and its scale. In the category (3), when a new good search point is found near the parent, parameters are adjusted to the direction of convergence. In problems with ridge landscape or multimodal landscape, where good search points exist in small region, parameters are tuned for small success and big success will be missed. Thus, search process would be trapped at a local optimal solution. In this study, we will pay attention to landscape such as ridge structure, which is independent of the problem scale, as the observation in the category (2).

3. Detecting Ridge Structure

In ridge structure, search points $\{x_i | i = 1, 2, \cdots, N\}$ will move through a narrow path, where $x_i = (x_{i1}, x_{i2}, \cdots, x_{iD})$ is a search point, D is the dimension of a point, and N is the number of search points. Figure 1 shows contour lines of a problem with ridge structure and search points (black circles). The points are moving toward the optimal solution (1,1). The best point will be nearest to the optimal solution.

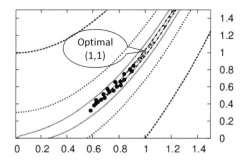

Figure 1. Contour lines and search points in a problem with ridge structure

Since the best point often locates at a front position of search points, the distance between the best point and the other point is large compared with the distance between a non-best point and the other points. Thus, two distance metrics of the best point compared with the other points can be defined as follows:

Ridge1 If the best point locates at a front of search points, average distance between the best point and the other points becomes large. Let $d_i, i = 1, 2, \cdots, N$ be the average distance between x_i and the other points. The ridge factor Rf_1 is defined by the average distance of the best point which is normalized in [0, 1]. When ridge structure is detected, the factor has a value near 1.

$$Rf_1 = \frac{d_{best} - d_{\min}}{d_{\max} - d_{\min}} \in [0, 1] \tag{5.1}$$

$$d_i = \frac{1}{N-1} \sum_{k=1, k \neq i}^{N} \sqrt{\sum_{j=1}^{D} (x_{ij} - x_{kj})^2}$$

where $d_{\min}$ and $d_{\max}$ are the minimum value and the maximum value of d_i, and d_{best} is the average distance of the best point. This metric is same as evolutionary factor defined in APSO [18].

Ridge2 If the best point locates at a front of search points, distance between the best point and a centroid g of all search points becomes large. Let $d_i, i = 1, 2, \cdots, N$ be the distance between x_i and the centroid. The ridge factor Rf_2 is defined by the distance of the best point which is normalized in [0, 1]. When ridge structure is detected, the factor has a value near 1.

$$Rf_2 = \frac{d_{best} - d_{\min}}{d_{\max} - d_{\min}} \in [0, 1] \tag{5.2}$$

$$g = \frac{1}{N} \sum_{i=1}^{N} x_i, \quad d_i = \sqrt{\sum_{j=1}^{D} (x_{ij} - g_j)^2}$$

where $d_{\min}$ and $d_{\max}$ are the minimum value and the maximum value of d_i, and d_{best} is the distance of the best point.

When search points are distributed around a narrow path, the correlation among variables becomes large. A correlation metric can be defined using eigen values of correlation matrix C as follows:

Ridge3 If there is no correlation among variables, all eigen values of the correlation matrix are 1. If there is strong correlation among variables, some eigen values have values much greater than 1. The ridge factor Rf_3 is define by relative value of the largest eigen value and the median eigen value. When ridge structure or correlation of variables is detected, the ridge factor has a value near 1.

$$Rf_3 = 1 - \frac{\lambda_{D/2}}{\lambda_1} \in [0, 1] \quad (5.3)$$

$$C_{ij} = \frac{\sum_{k=1}^{D}(x_{ik} - \bar{x}_k)(x_{jk} - \bar{x}_k)}{\sqrt{\sum_{k=1}^{D}(x_{ik} - \bar{x}_k)^2}\sqrt{\sum_{k=1}^{D}(x_{jk} - \bar{x}_k)^2}}$$

$$\bar{x}_k = \frac{1}{N}\sum_{i=1}^{N} x_{ik}$$

Eigen values of C are $\lambda_1 \geq \lambda_2 \geq \cdots \geq \lambda_D$.

The Rf_1, Rf_2 and Rf_3 values change very unstably. In order to realize stable control of algorithm parameters, exponential moving average of ridge factors is introduced:

$$Rf = (1 - C) \cdot Rf + C \cdot Rf' \quad (5.4)$$

where Rf' is a current Rf value, C is a weight for current value of ridge factor, and Rf is the moving average.

4. Differential Evolution with Detecting Ridge Structure

Optimization problems are defined and differential evolution is briefly explained because DE is used for comparing the performances of proposed methods for detecting ridge structure.

4.1 Optimization Problems

In this study, the following optimization problem with lower bound and upper bound constraints will be discussed.

$$\begin{aligned}&\text{minimize} \quad f(\boldsymbol{x}) \\ &\text{subject to} \quad l_i \leq x_i \leq u_i, \; i = 1, \ldots, D,\end{aligned} \quad (5.5)$$

where $\boldsymbol{x} = (x_1, x_2, \cdots, x_D)$ is a D dimensional vector and $f(\boldsymbol{x})$ is an objective function. The function f is a nonlinear real-valued function. Values l_i and u_i are the lower bound and the upper bound of x_i, respectively.

4.2 Differential Evolution

DE is an evolutionary algorithm proposed by Storn and Price [1,2]. DE has been successfully applied to the optimization problems including non-linear, non-differentiable, non-convex and multimodal functions. It has been shown that DE is fast and robust to these functions [19].

In DE, initial individuals are randomly generated within given search space and form an initial population. Each individual contains D genes as decision variables. At each generation or iteration, all individuals are selected as parents. Each parent is processed as follows: The mutation operation begins by choosing several individuals from the population except for the parent in the processing. The first individual is a base vector. All subsequent individuals are paired to create difference vectors. The difference vectors are scaled by a scaling factor F and added to the base vector. The resulting vector, or a mutant vector, is then recombined with the parent. The probability of recombination at an element is controlled by a crossover rate CR. This crossover operation produces a child, or a trial vector. Finally, for survivor selection, the trial vector is accepted for the next generation if the trial vector is better than the parent.

There are some variants of DE that have been proposed. The variants are classified using the notation DE/*base*/*num*/*cross* such as DE/rand/1/bin and DE/rand/1/exp.

"*base*" specifies a way of selecting an individual that will form the base vector. For example, DE/rand selects an individual for the base vector at random from the population. DE/best selects the best individual in the population.

"*num*" specifies the number of difference vectors used to perturb the base vector. In case of DE/rand/1, for example, for each parent x^i, three individuals x^{p1}, x^{p2} and x^{p3} are chosen randomly from the population without overlapping x^i and each other. A new vector, or a mutant vector x' is generated by the base vector x^{p1} and the difference vector $x^{p2} - x^{p3}$, where F is the scaling factor.

$$x' = x^{p1} + F(x^{p2} - x^{p3}) \tag{5.6}$$

"*cross*" specifies the type of crossover that is used to create a child. For example, 'bin' indicates that the crossover is controlled by the binomial crossover using a constant crossover rate, and 'exp' indicates that the crossover is controlled by a kind of two-point crossover using exponentially decreasing the crossover rate. Figure 2 shows the binomial and exponential crossover. A new child x^{child} is generated from the parent x^i and the mutant vector x', where CR is a crossover rate.

---

binomial crossover DE/·/·/bin
```
  j_rand=randint(1,D);
  for(k=1; k≤D; k++) {
    if(k==j_rand || u(0,1)<CR) x_k^child=x'_k;
    else x_k^child=x_k^i;
  }
```
exponential crossover DE/·/·/exp
```
  k=1; j=randint(1,D);
  do {
    x_j^child=x'_j;
    k=k+1; j=(j+1)%D;
  } while(k≤D && u(0,1)<CR);
  while(k≤D) {
    x_j^child=x_j^i;
    k=k+1; j=(j+1)%D;
  }
```

Figure 2. Binomial and exponential crossover operation, where randint(1,D) generates an integer randomly from $[1, D]$ and $u(l, r)$ is a uniform random number generator in $[l, r]$.

The algorithm of DE is as follows:

Step1 Initialization of a population. Initial N individuals $P = \{x^i, i = 1, 2, \cdots, N\}$ are generated randomly in search space and form an initial population.

Step2 Termination condition. If the number of function evaluations exceeds the maximum number of evaluation $FE_{\max}$, the algorithm is terminated.

Step3 DE operations. Each individual x^i is selected as a parent. If all individuals are selected, go to Step4. A mutant vector x' is generated according to Eq. (5.6). A trial vector (child) is generated from the parent x^i and the mutant vector x' using a crossover operation shown in Figure 2. If the child is better than or equal to the parent, or the DE operation is succeeded, the child survives. Otherwise the parent survives. Go back to Step3 and the next individual is selected as a parent.

Step4 Survivor selection (generation change). The population is organized by the survivors. Go back to Step2.

Figure 3 shows a pseudo-code of DE/rand/1.

```
DE/rand/1()
{
// Initialize an population
 P=N individuals generated randomly in S;
 for(t=1; FE ≤ FE_max; t++) {
  for(i=1; i ≤ N; i++) {
// DE operation
     x^p1=Randomly selected from P(p1 ≠ i);
     x^p2=Randomly selected from P(p2 ∉ {i,p1});
     x^p3=Randomly selected from P(p3 ∉ {i,p1,p2});
     x'=x^p1+F(x^p2 − x^p3);
     x^child=trial vector is generated from x^i and x'
         by the crossover operation;
// Survivor selection
     if(f(x^child) ≤ f(x^i))  z^i=x^child;
     else                     z^i=x^i;
     FE=FE+1;
  }
  P={z^i, i = 1, 2, ···, N};
 }
}
```

Figure 3. The pseudo-code of DE, FE is the number of function evaluations.

4.3 Parameter Control for Ridge Structure

As for the scaling factor F, global search is strengthened by increasing F and local search is strengthened by decreasing F. Global search is strengthened by increasing population size N and local search is strengthened by decreasing N. The scaling factor F and population size N are in a trade-off relation. Thus, large population size with small F and small population size with large F show similar results. The crossover rate CR controls the number of variables changed simultaneously. Small CR is effective to problems with separable variables and large CR is effective to problems with dependent variables.

In this study, F and CR are controlled based on ridge factor Rf. If Rf is small enough, F is decreased to strengthen local search and improve search efficiency. If Rf is large, F is increased to strengthen global search and keep diversity of search. Also, if Rf is small enough, CR is decreased somewhat, because it is thought that variables are not so correlated.

$$F = \begin{cases} F_0 - \alpha_{Rf}(Rf_{low} - Rf) & Rf < Rf_{low} \\ F_0 + \alpha_{Rf}(Rf - Rf_{high}) & Rf > Rf_{high} \\ F_0 & otherwise \end{cases} \quad (5.7)$$

$$CR = \begin{cases} CR_0 - \alpha_{Rf}(Rf_{low} - Rf) & Rf < Rf_{low} \\ CR_0 & otherwise \end{cases} \quad (5.8)$$

where F_0 and CR_0 are initial values of F and CR. Parameter values of Rf_{low}, Rf_{high} and α_{Rf} for Rf_1, Rf_2 and Rf_3 will be defined later.

Figure 4 shows a pseudo-code of DE/rand/1 with detecting ridge structure.

5. Numerical Experiments

In this paper, well-known thirteen benchmark problems are solved.

5.1 Test Problems

The 13 scalable benchmark functions are sphere, Schwefel 2.22, Schwefel 1.2, Schwefel 2.21, Rosenbrock, step, noisy quartic, Schwefel 2.26, Rastrigin, Ackley, Griewank, and two penalized functions, respectively [16, 20].

The function definitions and their search spaces, where D is the dimension of the decision vector, are as follows:

- f_1: Sphere function

$$f_1(\boldsymbol{x}) = \sum_{i=1}^{D} x_i^2, \quad -100 \leq x_i \leq 100 \quad (5.9)$$

The function f_1 is a unimodal and smooth function. The optimal solution is $\boldsymbol{x}_{\min} = (0, 0, \cdots, 0)$ and the minimum value is $f_1(\boldsymbol{x}_{\min}) = 0$.

- f_2: Schwefel 2.22 function

$$f_2(\boldsymbol{x}) = \sum_{i=1}^{D} |x_i| + \prod_{i=1}^{D} |x_i|, \quad -10 \leq x_i \leq 10 \quad (5.10)$$

The function f_2 is a unimodal and continuous function with some edges. The optimal solution is $\boldsymbol{x}_{\min} = (0, 0, \cdots, 0)$ and the minimum value is $f_2(\boldsymbol{x}_{\min}) = 0$.

```
DE/rand/1 with detecting ridge structure()
{
// Initialize an population
 P=N individuals generated randomly in S;
 for(t=1; FE ≤ FE_max; t++) {
  Rf' is obtained according to Eq. (5.1), (5.2) or (5.3);
  if(t==1)
      Rf=Rf';
  else
      Rf=(1-C)*Rf+C*Rf';
  if(Rf < Rf_low) {
      F=F_0 - α_Rf(Rf_low - Rf);
      CR=CR_0 - α_Rf(Rf_low - Rf);
  }
  else if(Rf > Rf_high) {
      F=F_0 + α_Rf(Rf - Rf_high);
      CR=CR_0;
  }
  else {
      F=F_0;
      CR=CR_0;
  }
  for(i=1; i ≤ N; i++) {
// DE operation
      x^{p1}=Randomly selected from P(p1 ≠ i);
      x^{p2}=Randomly selected from P(p2 ∉ {i,p1});
      x^{p3}=Randomly selected from P(p3 ∉ {i,p1,p2});
      x'=x^{p1}+F(x^{p2} - x^{p3});
      x^child=trial vector is generated from x^i and x'
           by the crossover operation;
// Survivor selection
      if(f(x^child) ≤ f(x^i))  z^i=x^child;
      else                     z^i=x^i;
      FE=FE+1;
  }
  P={z^i, i = 1, 2, ···, N};
 }
}
```

Figure 4. The pseudo-code of DE with detecting ridge structure

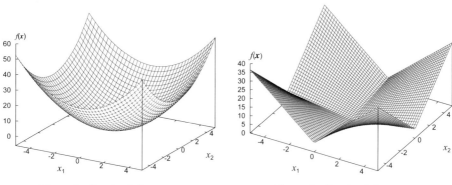

Figure 5. Graph of f_1 **Figure 6.** Graph of f_2

- f_3: Schwefel 1.2 function

$$f_3(\boldsymbol{x}) = \sum_{i=1}^{D} \left(\sum_{j=1}^{i} x_j \right)^2, \quad -100 \leq x_i \leq 100 \quad (5.11)$$

The function f_3 is a unimodal and smooth function. The optimal solution is $\boldsymbol{x}_{\min} = (0, 0, \cdots, 0)$ and the minimum value is $f_3(\boldsymbol{x}_{\min}) = 0$.

- f_4: Schwefel 2.21 function

$$f_4(\boldsymbol{x}) = \max_i \{|x_i|\}, \quad -100 \leq x_i \leq 100 \quad (5.12)$$

The function f_4 is a unimodal and continuous function with some edges The optimal solution is $\boldsymbol{x}_{\min} = (0, 0, \cdots, 0)$ and the minimum value is $f_4(\boldsymbol{x}_{\min}) = 0$.

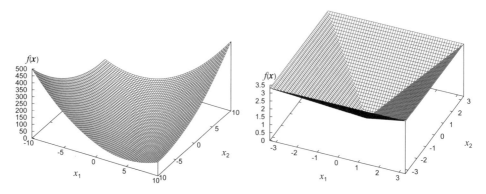

Figure 7. Graph of f_3 **Figure 8.** Graph of f_4

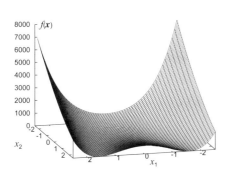
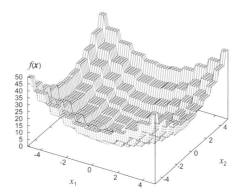

Figure 9. Graph of f_5 **Figure 10.** Graph of f_6

- f_5: Rosenbrock function

$$f_5(\boldsymbol{x}) = \sum_{i=1}^{D-1} \left[100(x_{i+1} - x_i^2)^2 + (x_i - 1)^2 \right], \quad -30 \leq x_i \leq 30 \quad (5.13)$$

The function f_5 is Rosenbrock function which is unimodal for 2- and 3-dimensions but may have multiple minima in high dimension cases [21]. The optimal solution is $\boldsymbol{x}_{\min} = (1, 1, \cdots, 1)$ and $f_5(\boldsymbol{x}_{\min}) = 0$.

- f_6: Step function

$$f_6(\boldsymbol{x}) = \sum_{i=1}^{D} \lfloor x_i + 0.5 \rfloor^2, \quad -100 \leq x_i \leq 100 \quad (5.14)$$

The function f_6 is a discontinuous step function. The optimal solution is $\boldsymbol{x}_{\min} = (0, 0, \cdots, 0)$ and $f_6(\boldsymbol{x}_{\min}) = 0$.

- f_7: Noisy quartic function

$$f_7(\boldsymbol{x}) = \sum_{i=1}^{D} i x_i^4 + rand[0, 1), \quad -1.28 \leq x_i \leq 1.28 \quad (5.15)$$

The function f_7 is a noisy quartic function. The optimal solution $\boldsymbol{x}_{\min} = (0, 0, \cdots, 0)$ and the minimum value is $f_7(\boldsymbol{x}_{\min}) = 0$

Functions f_8 to f_{13} are multimodal functions and the number of its local minima increases exponentially with the problem dimension D [22].

- f_8: Schwefel 2.26 function

$$f_8(\boldsymbol{x}) = \sum_{i=1}^{D} -x_i \sin \sqrt{|x_i|} + D \cdot 418.98288727243369, \quad -500 \leq x_i \leq 500 \quad (5.16)$$

The optimal solution $\boldsymbol{x}_{\min} = (420.9687, 420.9687, \cdots, 420.9687)$ and the minimum value $f_8(\boldsymbol{x}_{\min}) = 0$.

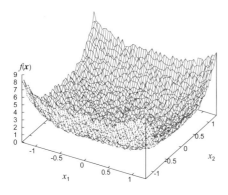
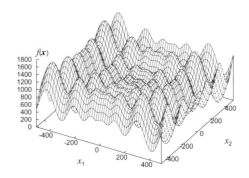

Figure 11. Graph of f_7 **Figure 12.** Graph of f_8

- f_9: Rastrigin function

$$f_9(\boldsymbol{x}) = \sum_{i=1}^{D} \left[x_i^2 - 10\cos(2\pi x_i) + 10 \right], \qquad -5.12 \leq x_i \leq 5.12 \qquad (5.17)$$

The optimal solution $\boldsymbol{x}_{\min} = (0, 0, \cdots, 0)$ and the minimum value is $f_9(\boldsymbol{x}_{\min}) = 0$

- f_{10}: Ackley function

$$f_{10}(\boldsymbol{x}) = -20\exp\left(-0.2\sqrt{\frac{1}{D}\sum_{i=1}^{D} x_i^2}\right) - \exp\left(\frac{1}{D}\sum_{i=1}^{D} \cos(2\pi x_i)\right) + 20 + e, \qquad (5.18)$$
$$-32 \leq x_i \leq 32$$

The optimal solution $\boldsymbol{x}_{\min} = (0, 0, \cdots, 0)$ and the minimum value is $f_{10}(\boldsymbol{x}_{\min}) = 0$

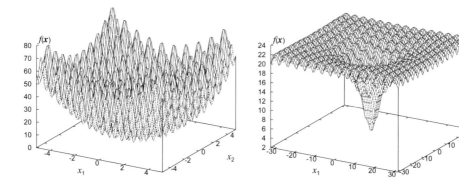

Figure 13. Graph of f_9 **Figure 14.** Graph of f_{10}

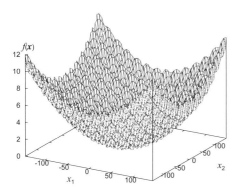
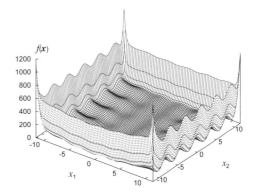

Figure 15. Graph of f_{11} **Figure 16.** Graph of f_{12}

- f_{11}: Griewank function

$$f_{11}(x) = \frac{1}{4000}\sum_{i=1}^{D} x_i^2 - \prod_{i=1}^{D}\cos\left(\frac{x_i}{\sqrt{i}}\right) + 1, \quad -600 \leq x_i \leq 600 \quad (5.19)$$

The optimal solution $x_{\min} = (0, 0, \cdots, 0)$ and the minimum value is $f_{11}(x_{\min}) = 0$

- f_{12}: Generalized Penalized function

$$\begin{aligned} f_{12}(x) &= \frac{\pi}{D}[10\sin^2(\pi y_1) + \sum_{i=1}^{D-1}(y_i - 1)^2\{1 + 10\sin^2(\pi y_{i+1})\} + (y_D - 1)^2] \\ &+ \sum_{i=1}^{D} u(x_i, 10, 100, 4), \quad -50 \leq x_i \leq 50 \end{aligned} \quad (5.20)$$

where

$$y_i = 1 + \frac{1}{4}(x_i + 1) \quad (5.21)$$

$$u(x_i, a, k, m) = \begin{cases} k(x_i - a)^m & x_i > a \\ 0 & -a \leq x_i \leq a \\ k(-x_i - a)^m & x_i < -a \end{cases} \quad (5.22)$$

The optimal solution $x_{\min} = (1, 1, \cdots, 1)$ and the minimum value is $f_{12}(x_{\min}) = 0$

- f_{13}: Generalized Penalized function

$$\begin{aligned} f_{13}(x) &= 0.1[\sin^2(3\pi x_1) + \sum_{i=1}^{D-1}(x_i - 1)^2\{1 + \sin^2(3\pi x_{i+1})\} \\ &+ (x_D - 1)^2\{1 + \sin^2(2\pi x_D)\}] + \sum_{i=1}^{D} u(x_i, 5, 100, 4), \\ &\quad -50 \leq x_i \leq 50 \end{aligned} \quad (5.23)$$

where $u(\cdot, \cdot, \cdot, \cdot)$ is given by (5.22).

The optimal solution $x_{\min} = (1, 1, \cdots, 1)$ and the minimum value is $f_{13}(x_{\min}) = 0$

Figures 21 $\sim$ 17 show the graphs of $f_1 \sim f_{13}$ in case of $D = 2$, respectively.

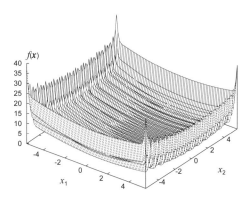

Figure 17. Graph of f_{13}

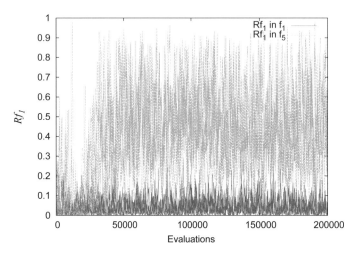

Figure 18. Graph of Rf_1 for f_1 and f_5 in 5 runs

5.2 Conditions of Experiments

The dimension of every problem is 30 (D=30). Experimental conditions are as follows: Parameters are population size $N = 50$, scaling factor $F = 0.5(= F_0)$ and crossover rate $CR = 0.9(= CR_0)$. Exponential crossover is adopted, because these settings showed very good and stable performance [23].

In order to determine parameters defined in Section 4.3, a typical unimodal problem f_1 and a typical problem with ridge structure f_5 are solved using DE/rand/1/exp with N=50, F=0.5 and CR=0.9 without controlling F and CR. Figures 18, 19 and 20 show the change of Rf_1, Rf_2 and Rf_3 values for f_1 and f_5 in 5 runs where the maximum number of function evaluations is 200,000.

From Figure 18, Rf_1 can be used to classify f_1 and f_5. In f_1, Rf_1 is almost between 0 and 0.1. In f_5, Rf_1 is almost between 0.2 and 0.8. From the result, Rf_{low}=0.1, Rf_{high}=0.4 and α_{Rf}=1 are selected.

From Figure 19, Rf_2 can be used to classify f_1 and f_5. In f_1, Rf_2 is almost between 0 and 0.15. In f_5, Rf_2 is almost between 0.25 and 0.85. From the result, Rf_{low}=0.15, Rf_{high}=0.45 and α_{Rf}=1 are selected.

From Figure 20, Rf_3 can be used to classify f_1 and f_5. In f_1, Rf_3 is almost between 0.75 and

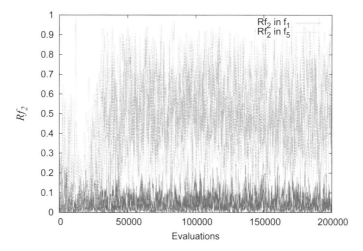

Figure 19. Graph of Rf_2 for f_1 and f_5 in 5 runs

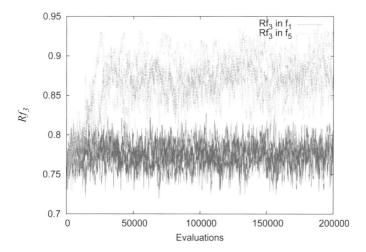

Figure 20. Graph of Rf_3 for f_1 and f_5 in 5 runs

0.85. In f_5, Rf_3 is almost between 0.85 and 0.9. From the result, Rf_{low}=0.8, Rf_{high}=0.85 and α_{Rf}=2.5 are selected. Also, the weight of current Rf for moving average C=0.2.

5.3 Experimental Results

In this paper, 50 independent runs are performed for 13 problems. Table 1 shows the experimental results on standard DE, DE with detecting ridge structure using Rf_1, Rf_2 and Rf_3. The mean value and the standard deviation of best objective value in 50 run are shown for each function. The maximum number of evaluations is selected for each function and is shown in column labeled $FE_{\max}$. The best result among algorithms is highlighted using bold face fonts.

As for f_1, f_2, f_9, f_{10}, f_{12} and f_{13}, DE with Rf_3 attained best average result followed by Rf_2, Rf_1 and standard DE. As for f_3, standard DE attained best average result followed by DE with Rf_1, Rf_2 and Rf_3. As for f_4, DE with Rf_3 attained best average result followed by Rf_1, Rf_2 and standard DE. As for f_5, DE with Rf_1 attained best average result followed by Rf_2, Rf_3 and standard DE. As for f_6 and f_8, all methods attained the same average result. As for f_7, DE with

Table 1. Experimental results on 13 functions

	FE_{max}	DE w.o. Rf	DE w. Rf_1	DE w. Rf_2	DE w. Rf_3
f_1	100,000	3.60e-24 ± 2.3e-24	7.86e-29 ± 5.7e-29	6.20e-31 ± 4.4e-31	**4.73e-31 ± 3.5e-31**
f_2	100,000	7.55e-14 ± 2.5e-14	6.41e-16 ± 2.9e-16	3.90e-17 ± 1.9e-17	**1.85e-18 ± 6.5e-19**
f_3	200,000	**4.42e-08 ± 4.2e-08**	1.98e-07 ± 1.2e-07	3.07e-07 ± 1.7e-07	1.42e-04 ± 1.1e-04
f_4	200,000	2.05e-05 ± 9.6e-06	1.77e-05 ± 7.6e-06	1.99e-05 ± 6.3e-06	**1.61e-05 ± 7.3e-06**
f_5	300,000	6.86e+00 ± 3.8e+00	**2.22e-25 ± 1.2e-24**	1.48e-24 ± 1.0e-23	3.51e-15 ± 3.9e-15
f_6	20,000	0.00e+00 ± 0.0e+00	0.00e+00 ± 0.0e+00	0.00e+00 ± 0.0e+00	0.00e+00 ± 0.0e+00
f_7	300,000	3.99e-03 ± 9.6e-04	3.85e-03 ± 1.0e-03	4.03e-03 ± 8.2e-04	**3.66e-03 ± 7.9e-04**
f_8	100,000	0.00e+00 ± 0.0e+00	0.00e+00 ± 0.0e+00	0.00e+00 ± 0.0e+00	**0.00e+00 ± 0.0e+00**
f_9	100,000	4.53e-06 ± 8.5e-06	2.57e-07 ± 1.0e-06	8.71e-08 ± 3.9e-07	**1.11e-07 ± 3.1e-08**
f_{10}	50,000	6.48e-06 ± 1.6e-06	5.25e-07 ± 1.2e-07	1.67e-07 ± 5.3e-08	**1.11e-07 ± 3.1e-08**
f_{11}	50,000	5.58e-09 ± 1.3e-08	2.72e-05 ± 1.3e-04	3.20e-10 ± 1.1e-09	**8.56e-12 ± 3.1e-11**
f_{12}	50,000	2.90e-11 ± 2.6e-11	4.26e-13 ± 3.8e-13	3.30e-14 ± 2.8e-14	**2.41e-15 ± 1.2e-15**
f_{13}	50,000	2.06e-10 ± 1.2e-10	2.11e-12 ± 1.9e-12	1.76e-13 ± 1.6e-13	**3.15e-14 ± 2.6e-14**

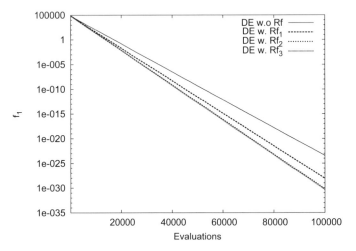

Figure 21. The convergence graph of f_1

Rf_3 attained best average result followed by DE with Rf_1, standard DE and DE with Rf_2. As for f_{11}, DE with Rf_3 attained best average result followed by Rf_2, standard DE and DE with Rf_1. Especially, DE with Rf_3 attained best average result in 9 functions out of 13 functions. Thus, it is thought that DE with Rf_3 is the best method among 4 methods.

Figures 21,22, 23, 24 and 25 show the change of best objective value found over the number of FEs within 100,000 evaluations. Apparently, proposed methods can find better objective values faster than or equivalent to standard DE in almost all problems except for f_3.

6. Conclusion

In this study, in order to solve difficult problems including problems with ridge structure effectively, three metrics (ridge factors) for detecting ridge structure are proposed: two ridge factors Rf_1 and Rf_2 using "distance relation between best point and the other points" and one ridge factor (Rf_3) using "correlation of variables". Also, adaptive control of algorithm parameters F and CR for DE is proposed according to the ridge factors.

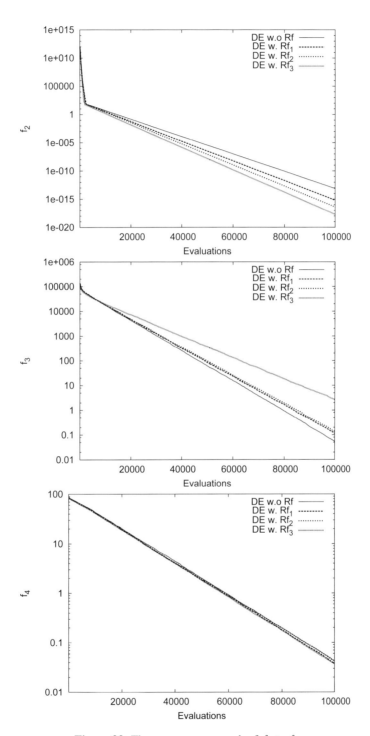

Figure 22. The convergence graph of f_2 to f_4

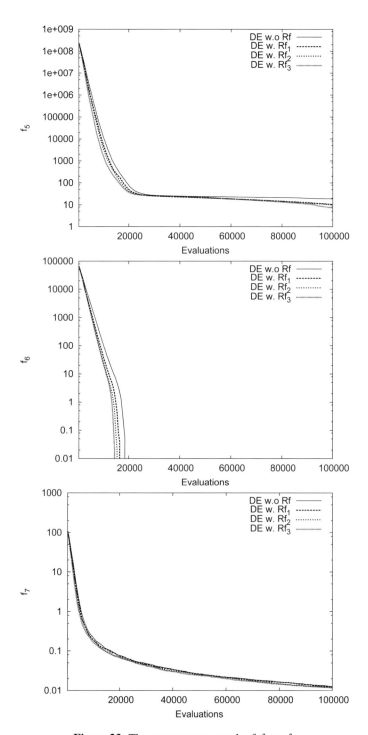

Figure 23. The convergence graph of f_5 to f_7

Detecting Ridge Structure for Population-Based Optimization Algorithms

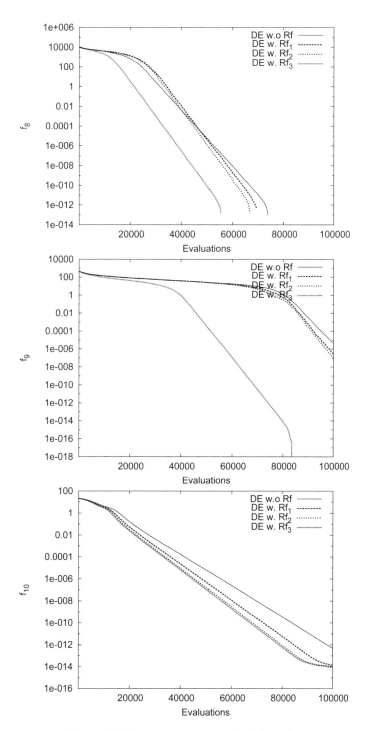

Figure 24. The convergence graph of f_8 to f_{10}

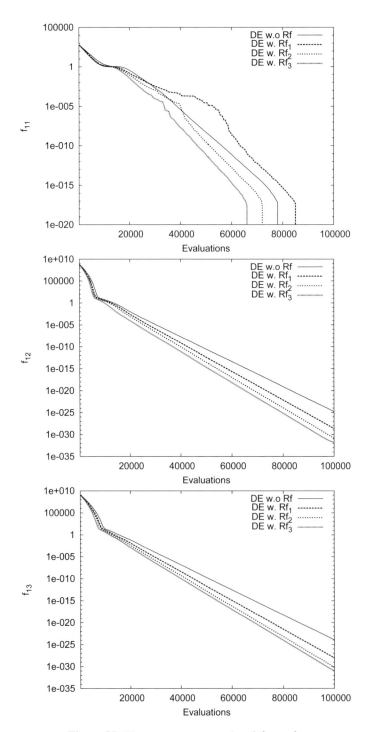

Figure 25. The convergence graphs of f_{11} to f_{13}

DE with controlling algorithm parameters based on the ridge factors is applied optimization of various 13 functions including unimodal functions, a function with ridge structure, multimodal functions. It is shown that the proposed method is effective compared with standard DE. Especially, three methods can solve a typical problem with ridge structure f_5 very efficiently.

In the future, we combine two types of parameter control: observation-based control such as ridge factor based control and success-based control to improve the efficiency and stability of POA including DE, PSO, and so on.

Acknowledgment

This study is supported by JSPS KAKENHI Grant Numbers 24500177 and 26350443.

References

[1] Storn, R. and Price, K., "Minimizing the Real Functions of the ICEC'96 Contest by Differential Evolution," *Proc. of the International Conference on Evolutionary Computation* (1996), pp. 842–844.

[2] Storn, R. and Price, K., "Differential Evolution – A Simple and Efficient Heuristic for Global Optimization over Continuous Spaces," *Journal of Global Optimization*, Vol. 11, pp. 341–359 (1997).

[3] Sakai, S. and Takahama, T., "A Comparative Study on Estimation Methods of Landscape Modality for Evolutionary Algorithms," M.Kitahara and C.Czerkawski (eds.), *Legal Informatics, Economic Science and Mathematical Research*, Kyushu University Press, pp. 55–80 (2014).

[4] Takahashi, R., Yata, N. and Nagao, T., "A Searching Algorithm Using Features of a Solution Space and Self-organizing Maps," *Transactions of the Institute of Electrical Engineers of Japan, C*, Vol. 131, No. 2 (2011), in Japanese.

[5] Takahama, T. and Sakai, S., "Differential Evolution with Dynamic Strategy and Parameter Selection by Detecting Landscape Modality," *Proc. of the 2012 IEEE Congress on Evolutionary Computation* (2012), pp. 2114–2121.

[6] Takahama, T. and Sakai, S., "Selecting Strategies in Particle Swarm Optimization by Sampling-Based Landscape Modality Detection," *Proc. of the 2014 International Conference on Parallel and Distributed Processing Techniques and Applications* (2014), pp. 215–221.

[7] Takahama, T. and Sakai, S., "Selecting Strategies in Particle Swarm Optimization by Sampling-Based Landscape Modality Detection Using Inner Products," *Proc. of the SICE Annual Conference 2014* (2014), pp. 1561–1566.

[8] Sakai, S. and Takahama, T., "A Comparative Study on Neighborhood Structures for Speciation in Species-Based Differential Evolution," M.Kitahara and C.Czerkawski (eds.), *Social Systems Solutions Applied by Economic Sciences and Mathematical Solutions,* Fukuoka: Kyushu University Press, pp. 111–135 (2012).

[9] Takahama, T. and Sakai, S., "Differential Evolution with Graph-Based Speciation by Competitive Hebbian Rules," *Proc. of the Sixth International Conference on Genetic and Evolutionary Computing (ICGEC2012)* (2012), pp. 445–448.

[10] Wang, Y., Cai, Z. and Zhang, Q., "Differential Evolution With Composite Trial Vector Generation Strategies and Control Parameters," *IEEE Transactions on Evolutionary Computation*, Vol. 15, No. 1, pp. 55–66 (2011).

[11] Liu, J. and Lampinen, J., "A Fuzzy Adaptive Differential Evolution Algorithm," *Soft Comput.*, Vol. 9, No. 6, pp. 448–462 (2005).

[12] Takahama, T. and Sakai, S., "Fuzzy C-Means Clustering and Partition Entropy for Species-Best Strategy and Search Mode Selection in Nonlinear Optimization by Differential Evolu-

tion," *Proc. of the 2011 IEEE International Conference on Fuzzy Systems* (2011), pp. 290–297.

[13] Teo, J., "Exploring Dynamic Self-Adaptive Populations in Differential Evolution," *Soft Comput.*, Vol. 10, No. 8, pp. 673–686 (2006).

[14] Qin, A., Huang, V. and Suganthan, P., "Differential Evolution Algorithm With Strategy Adaptation for Global Numerical Optimization," *IEEE Transactions on Evolutionary Computation*, Vol. 13, No. 2, pp. 398–417 (2009).

[15] Brest, J., Greiner, S., Boskovic, B., Mernik, M. and Zumer, V., "Self-Adapting Control Parameters in Differential Evolution: A Comparative Study on Numerical Benchmark Problems," *IEEE Transaction on Evolutionary Computation*, Vol. 10, No. 6, pp. 646–657 (2006).

[16] Zhang, J. and Sanderson, A. C., "JADE: Adaptive Differential Evolution With Optional External Archive," *IEEE Transactions on Evolutionary Computation*, Vol. 13, No. 5, pp. 945–958 (2009).

[17] Islam, S. M., Das, S., Ghosh, S., Roy, S. and Suganthan, P. N., "An Adaptive Differential Evolution Algorithm With Novel Mutation and Crossover Strategies for Global Numerical Optimization," *IEEE Transactions on Systems, Man, and Cybernetics, Part B: Cybernetics*, Vol. 42, No. 2, pp. 482–500 (2012).

[18] Zhan, Z.-H., Zhang, J., Li, Y. and Chung, H. S.-H., "Adaptive particle swarm optimization," *IEEE Transactions on Systems, Man, and Cybernetics, Part B: Cybernetics*, Vol. 39, No. 6, pp. 1362–1381 (2009).

[19] Chakraborty, U. K. (ed.), *Advances in Differential Evolution*, Springer (2008).

[20] Yao, X., Liu, Y., Liang, K.-H. and Lin, G., "Fast Evolutionary Algorithms," Ghosh, A. and Tsutsui, S. (eds.), *Advances in Evolutionary Computing: Theory and Applications*, New York, NY, USA: Springer-Verlag New York, Inc., pp. 45–94 (2003).

[21] Shang, Y.-W. and Qiu, Y.-H., "A Note on the Extended Rosenbrock Function," *Evolutionary Computation*, Vol. 14, No. 1, pp. 119–126 (2006).

[22] Yao, X., Liu, Y. and Liu, G., "Evolutionary Programming Made Faster,", *IEEE Trans. on Evolutionary Computation*, Vol. 3, No. 2, pp. 82–102 (1999).

[23] Takahama, T. and Sakai, S., "Fast and Stable Constrained Optimization by the ε Constrained Differential Evolution," *Pacific Journal of Optimization*, Vol. 5, No. 2, pp. 261–282 (2009).

Chapter 6

Explicit Irreducible Decomposition of Harmonic Polynomials in the Case of $\mathfrak{so}(p,2)$

Ryoko Wada and Yoshio Agaoka**
*Faculty of Economic Sciences, Hiroshima Shudo University,
1-1 Ozuka-Higashi 1-chome, Asaminami-Ku, Hiroshima, Japan 731-3195,
**Department of Mathematics, Graduate School of Science, Hiroshima University,
7-1 Kagamiyama 1-chome, Higashi-Hiroshima, Japan 739-8521.

Abstract
Concerning classical harmonic polynomials on $\mathbf{C}^p$, many results have been obtained from several standpoints. For example, Kostant-Rallis treated this subject from the Lie algebraic viewpoint, and considered the classical harmonic polynomials on $\mathbf{C}^p$ as polynomials on some specific vector space, which is canonically associated with the Lie algebra $\mathfrak{so}(p,1)$. In the series of papers we further investigate harmonic polynomials from their standpoint for the Lie algebras $\mathfrak{su}(p,1)$, $\mathfrak{sp}(p,1)$ and $\mathfrak{f}_{4(-20)}$. In particular in the previous paper we considered harmonic polynomials for the real rank 2 case $\mathfrak{so}(p,2)$, and obtained the formula of irreducible decomposition in the character level. In this paper we explain a method to decompose the space of harmonic polynomials into irreducible factors, and we explicitly give its decomposition for low degree cases.

Key Words:
Harmonic polynomial, Spherical harmonics, Reproducing kernel, Special function

1. Introduction

This is a continuation of our previous papers [10], [11].

Let $\mathfrak{g}$ be a complex semisimple Lie algebra and let $\mathfrak{g}_\mathbf{R}$ be a noncompact real form of $\mathfrak{g}$. We fix a maximal compact subalgebra $\mathfrak{k}_\mathbf{R}$ of $\mathfrak{g}_\mathbf{R}$, and let $\mathfrak{g}_\mathbf{R} = \mathfrak{k}_\mathbf{R} + \mathfrak{p}_\mathbf{R}$ be a Cartan decomposition of $\mathfrak{g}_\mathbf{R}$. We denote by $\mathfrak{g} = \mathfrak{k} + \mathfrak{p}$ its complexification.

In [8], [9] we considered the reproducing formulas of the harmonic polynomials in the cases where $\mathfrak{g}_\mathbf{R}$'s are of real rank 1, and in [10], we considered the case $\mathfrak{g}_\mathbf{R} = \mathfrak{so}(p,2)$, which is the case of the classical real rank 2. (For details of harmonic theory on $\mathfrak{p}$, see Kostant-Rallis [5].) We explicitly gave the $\mathfrak{k}_\mathbf{R}$-irreducible decomposition of the space of harmonic polynomials of degree ≤ 4, including their generators, and showed the reproducing formulas for some cases.

In [11], we gave the $\mathfrak{k}_\mathbf{R}$-irreducible decomposition of the space of harmonic polynomials of general dimension in the case $\mathfrak{g}_\mathbf{R} = \mathfrak{so}(p,2)$ and give the examples of reproducing formulas of harmonic polynomials of degree ≤ 4.

In this paper, we will give an algorithm to obtain the generators of irreducible components of the space of harmonic polynomials for the case $\mathfrak{g}_\mathbf{R} = \mathfrak{so}(p, 2)$. For this purpose we show the structure theorem of the $\mathfrak{k}_\mathbf{R}$-irreducible decomposition of the space of polynomials on $\mathfrak{p}$. Explicit decomposition and generators are listed up for degree ≤ 5.

Furthermore, we will give the reproducing formulas of the principal part of the spaces of harmonic polynomials of degree ≤ 5.

2. Preliminaries

In this section we fix several notations and review some definitions. For details, see our previous papers [10], [11]. Let p be an integer with $p \geq 3$ and n be a non-negative integer. We denote by $H_n(\mathbf{C}^p)$ the space of harmonic polynomials on $\mathbf{C}^p$ of degree n, i.e., the space of polynomials f on $\mathbf{C}^p$ of degree n satisfying $\sum_{j=1}^{p} \frac{\partial^2}{\partial z_j^2} f(z) = 0$. We denote by $H_{n,p}$ the space of spherical harmonics of degree n in dimension p, i.e., $H_{n,p} = H_n(\mathbf{C}^p)|_{S^{p-1}}$, where S^{p-1} is the unit sphere in $\mathbf{R}^p$.

For $z, w \in \mathbf{C}^p$ we put $z \cdot w = {}^t z w$, $z^2 = z \cdot z$, $w^2 = w \cdot w$. Then the natural action of the special orthogonal group $SO(p)$ preserves this product.

Now let $\mathfrak{g} = \mathfrak{k} + \mathfrak{p}$, $\mathfrak{g}_\mathbf{R} = \mathfrak{k}_\mathbf{R} + \mathfrak{p}_\mathbf{R}$ be direct sum decompositions as stated in Introduction. We put $K = \exp \operatorname{ad} \mathfrak{k} \subset GL(\mathfrak{p})$ and $K_\mathbf{R} = \exp \operatorname{ad} \mathfrak{k}_\mathbf{R}$.

Let $S(\mathfrak{p})$ be the symmetric algebra over $\mathfrak{p}$ and let S be the space of polynomials on $\mathfrak{p}$. For $X \in \mathfrak{p}$ we denote by $\partial(X)$ the differential operator defined by

$$(\partial(X)f)(Y) = \frac{d}{dt}f(Y + tX)|_{t=0} \qquad (f \in S,\ Y \in \mathfrak{p}).$$

The mapping $X \mapsto \partial(X)$ naturally extends to an isomorphism of $S(\mathfrak{p})$ onto the algebra of all differential operators on $\mathfrak{p}$ with complex coefficients. For $f \in S$ and $g \in K$, we define an element $\rho(g)f$ of S by $\rho(g)f(X) = f(g^{-1}X)$ for $X \in \mathfrak{p}$. Let J denote the ring of K-invariant polynomials on $\mathfrak{p}$ and we put $J_+ = \{f \in J;\ f(0) = 0\}$.

Let $I(\mathfrak{p})$ be the set of K-invariants of $S(\mathfrak{p})$ and we put $I_+(\mathfrak{p}) = \{u \in I(\mathfrak{p})\ ;\ \partial(u)1 = 0\}$, i.e., $I_+(\mathfrak{p}) \subset I(\mathfrak{p})$ is the set of K-invariants without constant term.

According to the definition in [5], $f \in S$ is harmonic if and only if $\partial(u)f = 0$ for any $u \in I_+(\mathfrak{p})$. We denote by S_n the space of homogeneous polynomials on $\mathfrak{p}$ of degree n, and $\mathcal{H}_n$ the space of homogeneous harmonic polynomials of degree n. Remark that K acts on S_n and $\mathcal{H}_n$. We regard $K_\mathbf{R} \subset K$ and $\mathfrak{p}_\mathbf{R} \subset \mathfrak{p}$ in the following. For more details on harmonic polynomials of $\mathfrak{p}$, see [2], [5].

Now we consider the case $\mathfrak{g}_\mathbf{R} = \mathfrak{so}(p, 2)$. From now we assume $p \geq 4$. We have

$$\mathfrak{k} = \left\{ \begin{pmatrix} A & 0 \\ 0 & B \end{pmatrix} \in M(p+2, \mathbf{C})\ ;\ A \in \mathfrak{so}(p, \mathbf{C}),\ B \in \mathfrak{so}(2, \mathbf{C}) \right\},$$

$$\mathfrak{p} = \left\{ \begin{pmatrix} 0 & X \\ {}^t X & 0 \end{pmatrix} \in M(p+2, \mathbf{C})\ ;\ X \text{ is a complex } p \times 2 \text{ matrix} \right\},$$

$$K_\mathbf{R} = \left\{ \operatorname{Ad} \begin{pmatrix} A & 0 \\ 0 & B \end{pmatrix}\ ;\ A \in SO(p)\, ,\ B \in SO(2) \right\},$$

and $\mathfrak{g} = \mathfrak{k} + \mathfrak{p}$. For $\widetilde{X} = \begin{pmatrix} 0 & X \\ {}^t X & 0 \end{pmatrix} \in \mathfrak{p}$, and $g = \operatorname{Ad} \begin{pmatrix} A & 0 \\ 0 & B \end{pmatrix} \in K_\mathbf{R}$ ($A \in SO(p), B \in SO(2)$) we have $g\widetilde{X} = \begin{pmatrix} 0 & AX{}^t B \\ {}^t(AX{}^t B) & 0 \end{pmatrix}$. For $\widetilde{X} = \begin{pmatrix} 0 & X \\ {}^t X & 0 \end{pmatrix} \in \mathfrak{p}$ with

$X = (x \ y) \ (x, y \in \mathbf{C}^p)$, two polynomials

$$P(\widetilde{X}) = \frac{1}{2} \operatorname{Tr}(\widetilde{X}^2) = x^2 + y^2, \quad Q(\widetilde{X}) = \det({}^t X X) = x^2 y^2 - (x \cdot y)^2$$

give the generators of J. Then we have $\mathcal{H}_n = \{f \in S_n; P(D)f = Q(D)f = 0\}$, where

$$P(D) = \Delta_x + \Delta_y, \quad Q(D) = \Delta_x \Delta_y - \left(\sum_{j=1}^{p} \frac{\partial^2}{\partial x_j \partial y_j}\right)^2,$$

$$\Delta_x = \sum_{j=1}^{p} \left(\frac{\partial}{\partial x_j}\right)^2, \ \Delta_y = \sum_{j=1}^{p} \left(\frac{\partial}{\partial y_j}\right)^2.$$

For $\widetilde{X} = \begin{pmatrix} 0 & X \\ {}^t X & 0 \end{pmatrix} \in \mathfrak{p}$ with $X = (x \ y) \ (x, y \in \mathbf{C}^p)$, we put $\begin{pmatrix} z \\ w \end{pmatrix} = \begin{pmatrix} x+iy \\ x-iy \end{pmatrix} \in \mathbf{C}^{2p}$ and we define the linear bijective mapping $\Psi : \mathfrak{p} \longrightarrow \mathbf{C}^{2p}$ by $\Psi(\widetilde{X}) = \begin{pmatrix} z \\ w \end{pmatrix}$. We denote by $S_n(\mathbf{C}^{2p})$ the space of homogeneous polynomials on $\mathbf{C}^{2p}$ with degree n and we put

$$\mathcal{H}_n(\mathbf{C}^{2p}) = \left\{ f\left(\begin{pmatrix} z \\ w \end{pmatrix}\right) \in S_n(\mathbf{C}^{2p}); \ \Delta_z \Delta_w f = 0 \text{ and } \Sigma_{j=1}^{p} \frac{\partial^2 f}{\partial z_j \partial w_j} = 0 \right\}.$$

Since we have $P(\widetilde{X}) = P \circ \Psi^{-1}\left(\begin{pmatrix} z \\ w \end{pmatrix}\right) = z \cdot w$ and $Q(\widetilde{X}) = Q \circ \Psi^{-1}\left(\begin{pmatrix} z \\ w \end{pmatrix}\right) = \frac{1}{4}\{z^2 w^2 - (z \cdot w)^2\}$, we can see that $f \in \mathcal{H}_n$ if and only if $f \circ \Psi^{-1} \in \mathcal{H}_n(\mathbf{C}^{2p})$.

3. Irreducible Decomposition of S_n

To obtain the explicit $K_{\mathbf{R}}$-irreducible decomposition of the space of harmonic polynomials $\mathcal{H}_n$, we first consider the $K_{\mathbf{R}}$-irreducible decomposition of the space S_n. In this section we review some fundamental facts on S_n and fix several notations. Concerning the space $\mathcal{H}_n$, we give an algorithms to obtain its explicit decomposition in §4.

We follow the notations given in [10, 11]. We first remark that the Lie group $K_{\mathbf{R}}$ is isomorphic to the product group $SO(p) \times SO(2)$. The highest weight of the irreducible representation of the group $SO(p)$ is expressed as $\sum n_i \Lambda_i$, where $\Lambda_1 \sim \Lambda_p$ are fundamental highest weights. The $SO(2)$-irreducible space is always 1-dimensional, and we express it simply as V_k, where k is some integer. Then in our case the irreducible component of $K_{\mathbf{R}}$ is symbolically expressed as $(n_1 \Lambda_1 + n_2 \Lambda_2) \otimes V_k$, where n_1, n_2 are non-negative integers and $k \in \mathbf{Z}$.

We first decompose the space S_n into $GL(p, \mathbf{C}) \times GL(2, \mathbf{C})$-irreducible components in the character level. As in [11] we denote the Schur function corresponding to the partition $n = n_1 + n_2 + \cdots + n_p$ $(n_1 \geq n_2 \geq \cdots \geq n_p \geq 0)$ by $T_{n_1, n_2, \cdots, n_p}$. In the same way we denote the character of the group $GL(2, \mathbf{C})$ by U_{ab} $(n = a+b, a \geq b \geq 0)$. Then, the space S_n is isomorphic to the space $S^n(\mathbf{C}^p \otimes \mathbf{C}^2)$ as a $GL(p, \mathbf{C}) \times GL(2, \mathbf{C})$-representation space, and hence its $GL(p, \mathbf{C}) \times GL(2, \mathbf{C})$-irreducible decomposition is given by

$$S_n = T_n U_n + T_{n-1,1} U_{n-1,1} + T_{n-2,2} U_{n-2,2} + \cdots$$
$$+ \begin{cases} T_{\frac{n+1}{2}, \frac{n-1}{2}} U_{\frac{n+1}{2}, \frac{n-1}{2}} & (n \text{ is odd}), \\ T_{\frac{n}{2}, \frac{n}{2}} U_{\frac{n}{2}, \frac{n}{2}} & (n \text{ is even}). \end{cases}$$

Next we apply the branching rules to the irreducible components T_{ab} and U_{ab} ($a + b = n$, $a \geq b$). The $SO(2)$-irreducible decomposition of the space U_{ab} is simply given by

$$U_{ab} = V_{a-b} + V_{a-b-2} + V_{a-b-4} + \cdots + V_{-(a-b)}$$

with dim $V_k = 1$. As for the $SO(p)$-irreducible decomposition of the space T_{ab}, we apply the theory of Koike-Terada [4] and the Littlewood-Richardson rule. The result is already given in [11; p.129]:

$$T_{ab} = \sum_{\begin{cases} 0 \leq p \leq a, \, 0 \leq q \leq b, \\ 0 \leq r \leq p, q, \\ p - r \leq a - b, \\ p \equiv a, \, q \equiv b \pmod 2 \end{cases}} \{(p + q - 2r)\Lambda_1 + r\Lambda_2\}.$$

Combining these formulas, we have the $SO(p) \times SO(2)$-irreducible decomposition of the space S_n. For example, in the case $n = 5$, we have

$$S_5 = T_5 U_5 + T_{41} U_{41} + T_{32} U_{32}$$
$$= \{(5\Lambda_1) + (3\Lambda_1) + (\Lambda_1)\} \otimes (V_5 + V_3 + V_1 + V_{-1} + V_{-3} + V_{-5})$$
$$+ \{(3\Lambda_1 + \Lambda_2) + (3\Lambda_1) + (\Lambda_1 + \Lambda_2) + (\Lambda_1)\} \otimes (V_3 + V_1 + V_{-1} + V_{-3})$$
$$+ \{(\Lambda_1 + 2\Lambda_2) + (3\Lambda_1) + (\Lambda_1 + \Lambda_2) + (\Lambda_1)\} \otimes (V_1 + V_{-1}).$$

Actually, we must expand these expressions to obtain the final irreducible decomposition such as

$$S_5 = (5\Lambda_1) \otimes V_5 + (5\Lambda_1) \otimes V_3 + \cdots + (3\Lambda_1 + \Lambda_2) \otimes V_3 + \cdots + (\Lambda_1) \otimes V_{-1}.$$

Thus, S_5 is decomposed into a sum of 42 $SO(p) \times SO(2)$-irreducible subspaces.

Now we introduce two important concepts. We say that the irreducible component $(p\Lambda_1 + q\Lambda_2) \otimes V_k$ in S_n is *principal* if $p + 2q = n$. Otherwise, we say it is a *lower* component of S_n. We denote by P_n the direct sum of principal irreducible components of S_n. For example, principal irreducible components of S_5 consists of 12 terms:

$$P_5 = (5\Lambda_1) \otimes (V_5 + V_3 + V_1 + V_{-1} + V_{-3} + V_{-5})$$
$$+ (3\Lambda_1 + \Lambda_2) \otimes (V_3 + V_1 + V_{-1} + V_{-3}) + (\Lambda_1 + 2\Lambda_2) \otimes (V_1 + V_{-1}).$$

(Compare with the decomposition of S_5 above.) Lower components of S_n may be obtained as follows: The 1-dimensional irreducible subspaces of quadratic polynomials S_2 are exhausted by

$$\{z^2\}, \quad \{z \cdot w\}, \quad \{w^2\},$$

whose characters are respectively given by
$$(0) \otimes V_2, \quad (0) \otimes V_0, \quad (0) \otimes V_{-2}.$$

Now we consider a principal component $(p\Lambda_1 + q\Lambda_2) \otimes V_k$ ($p + 2q = n - 2l$) of S_{n-2l} ($0 < l \leq n/2$). Then by making a tensor product with an l-th product of the above three quadratic polynomials $(z^2)^s (z \cdot w)^t (w^2)^u$ ($s + t + u = l$), we obtain a lower irreducible component $(p\Lambda_1 + q\Lambda_2) \otimes V_{k+2s-2u}$ in S_n. In the following, we express this irreducible component of S_n symbolically as
$$(p\Lambda_1 + q\Lambda_2) \otimes V_{k+[s,t,u]}.$$

We denote by L_n the subspace of S_n consisting of lower components of S_n. For example, we have
$$\begin{aligned} L_5 = &\{(3\Lambda_1) + (\Lambda_1)\} \otimes (V_5 + V_3 + V_1 + V_{-1} + V_{-3} + V_{-5}) \\ &+ \{(3\Lambda_1) + (\Lambda_1 + \Lambda_2) + (\Lambda_1)\} \otimes (V_3 + V_1 + V_{-1} + V_{-3}) \\ &+ \{(3\Lambda_1) + (\Lambda_1 + \Lambda_2) + (\Lambda_1)\} \otimes (V_1 + V_{-1}). \end{aligned}$$

Any irreducible component of L_n can be essentially obtained in this way, as the following structure theorem of S_n shows.

Theorem 3.1. *The $SO(p) \times SO(2)$-irreducible decomposition of S_n is given by:*

$$S_n = \sum_{\substack{p+2q+2(s+t+u)=n, \\ p \geq 0, q \geq 0, \\ s \geq 0, t \geq 0, u \geq 0}} (p\Lambda_1 + q\Lambda_2) \otimes (V_{p+[s,t,u]} + V_{p-2+[s,t,u]} + \cdots + V_{-(p-2)+[s,t,u]} + V_{-p+[s,t,u]}),$$

where we consider $(p\Lambda_1 + q\Lambda_2) \otimes V_{k+[s,t,u]} = (p\Lambda_1 + q\Lambda_2) \otimes V_k$ in case $p + 2q = n$ and $s = t = u = 0$.

In particular, the irreducible decompositions of the principal part P_n and the lower part L_n are respectively given by:

$$P_n = \sum_{\substack{p+2q=n, \\ p \geq 0, q \geq 0}} (p\Lambda_1 + q\Lambda_2) \otimes (V_p + V_{p-2} + \cdots + V_{-(p-2)} + V_{-p})$$

and

$$L_n = \sum_{\substack{p+2q<n, \\ p \equiv n \pmod{2}, \\ p \geq 0, q \geq 0, \\ s+t+u=(n-p-2q)/2, \\ s \geq 0, t \geq 0, u \geq 0}} (p\Lambda_1 + q\Lambda_2) \otimes (V_{p+[s,t,u]} + V_{p-2+[s,t,u]} + \cdots + V_{-(p-2)+[s,t,u]} + V_{-p+[s,t,u]}).$$

As a consequence, the lower part L_n is a direct sum of irreducible subspaces each of which is a tensor product of some irreducible principal component of low degree $S_{n-2(s+t+u)}$ and a product of quadratic polynomials $(z^2)^s (z \cdot w)^t (w^2)^u$.

Any polynomial in the principal component P_n is harmonic, and the multiplicity of any irreducible principal component is 1.

Generally, the multiplicity of the irreducible component $(p\Lambda_1 + q\Lambda_2) \otimes V_k$ in S_n can be obtained by the following generating function: Assume $p + 2q \le n$, $|k| \le n$ and $p \equiv n \equiv k \pmod 2$. Then the multiplicity of the irreducible component $(p\Lambda_1 + q\Lambda_2) \otimes V_k$ of S_n is equal to the coefficient of z^k in

$$\frac{(1-z^{2l+2})(1-z^{2l+4})(1-z^{2p+2})}{z^{p+2l}(1-z^2)^2(1-z^4)},$$

where $2l = n - p - 2q$.

Roughly speaking, we may say that the polynomial ring $\sum_n S_n$ is generated symbolically by the principal components P_n and three quadratic polynomials z^2, $z \cdot w$, w^2. Remark that the above expression $(p\Lambda_1 + q\Lambda_2) \otimes (V_p + \cdots + V_{-p})$ etc. actually means the direct sum

$$(p\Lambda_1 + q\Lambda_2) \otimes V_p + \cdots + (p\Lambda_1 + q\Lambda_2) \otimes V_{-p}.$$

Proof. We first consider the decomposition

$$S_n = T_n U_n + T_{n-1,1} U_{n-1,1} + \cdots + T_{ab} U_{ab} + \cdots.$$

Then, for $a + b = n$ and $a \ge b \ge 0$, we have the decomposition

$$T_{ab} = \sum_{\begin{cases} 0 \le p \le a,\ 0 \le q \le b, \\ 0 \le r \le p, q, \\ p - r \le a - b, \\ p \equiv a,\ q \equiv b \pmod 2 \end{cases}} \{(p + q - 2r)\Lambda_1 + r\Lambda_2\},$$

as stated before. If $(p + q - 2r) + 2r = n$, then we have $p + q = n = a + b$, and hence $p = a$, $q = b$ and $r = b$. Thus the principal part in $T_{ab} U_{ab}$ is given by $\{(a-b)\Lambda_1 + b\Lambda_2\} \otimes (V_{a-b} + \cdots + V_{-(a-b)})$. Hence the principal part P_n is expressed in the form

$$P_n = \sum_{\begin{cases} p + 2q = n, \\ p \ge 0, q \ge 0 \end{cases}} (p\Lambda_1 + q\Lambda_2) \otimes (V_p + V_{p-2} + \cdots + V_{-(p-2)} + V_{-p}).$$

It is easy to see that the number of irreducible components of P_n is equal to

$$\begin{cases} \frac{1}{4}(n+1)(n+3) & (n \text{ is odd}), \\ \frac{1}{4}(n+2)^2 & (n \text{ is even}). \end{cases}$$

Next we count the number of irreducible components appearing in the direct sum

$$\sum_{\begin{cases} p + 2q + 2(s+t+u) = n, \\ p \ge 0, q \ge 0, \\ s \ge 0, t \ge 0, u \ge 0 \end{cases}} (p\Lambda_1 + q\Lambda_2) \otimes (V_{p+[s,t,u]} + V_{p-2+[s,t,u]} + \cdots + V_{-(p-2)+[s,t,u]} + V_{-p+[s,t,u]}).$$

The total number of monomials of the form $(z^2)^s(z \cdot w)^t(w^2)^u$ with fixed $l = s+t+u$ is equal to ${}_3H_l = (l+1)(l+2)/2$. In case n is odd, the number of the principal irreducible components of P_{n-2l} is $(n-2l+1)(n-2l+3)/4$. Thus the total number of the above direct sum is equal to

$$\sum_{l=0}^{\frac{n-1}{2}} \frac{1}{4}(n-2l+1)(n-2l+3) \cdot \frac{1}{2}(l+1)(l+2)$$
$$= \frac{1}{1920}(n+1)(n+3)(n+5)(n+7)(n+9).$$

Similarly, in case n is even, the total number is equal to

$$\frac{1}{1920}(n+2)(n+4)(n+5)(n+6)(n+8)$$
$$= \frac{1}{1920}n(n+2)(n+4)(n+6)(n+8) + \frac{1}{384}(n+2)(n+4)(n+6)(n+8).$$

Next, we count the number of irreducible components of S_n. If this number coincides with the above number just obtained, then we have proved the decomposition formula of the space S_n in Theorem 3.1. For this purpose we use the following formula of Kostant-Rallis [5]:

$$S_n = \mathcal{H}_n \oplus (J_+ S)_n$$

(for details, see [10; p.83]). Applying this formula repeatedly, we obtain the direct sum decomposition

$$S_n \cong \mathcal{H}_n + \mathcal{H}_{n-2} + 2\left(\mathcal{H}_{n-4} + \mathcal{H}_{n-6}\right) + 3\left(\mathcal{H}_{n-8} + \mathcal{H}_{n-10}\right) + \cdots$$
$$+ \begin{cases} \frac{n}{4}(\mathcal{H}_4 + \mathcal{H}_2) + \frac{n+4}{4}\mathcal{H}_0 & (n \equiv 0 \pmod 4), \\ \frac{n-1}{4}(\mathcal{H}_5 + \mathcal{H}_3) + \frac{n+3}{4}\mathcal{H}_1 & (n \equiv 1 \pmod 4), \\ \frac{n+2}{4}(\mathcal{H}_2 + \mathcal{H}_0) & (n \equiv 2 \pmod 4), \\ \frac{n+1}{4}(\mathcal{H}_3 + \mathcal{H}_1) & (n \equiv 3 \pmod 4), \end{cases}$$

as a representation space. We have already known the formula of the number of irreducible components of $\mathcal{H}_n$:

$$\begin{cases} \frac{1}{12}(n+1)(n+2)(n+3) & (n \text{ is odd}) \\ \frac{1}{12}(n+2)(n^2+4n+6) & (n \text{ is even}) \end{cases}$$

(cf. [11; p.127]). Combining these formulas, we can calculate the number of irreducible components of S_n for two cases n is odd and even. After some calculations, we know that the results just coincide with the numbers we obtained above.

Next, we determine the generating function expressing the multiplicity of the component $(p\Lambda_1 + q\Lambda_2) \otimes V_k$ in S_n for fixed p and q. We put $2l = n - p - 2q$, and consider the principal part of S_{n-2l} with character $(p\Lambda_1 + q\Lambda_2) \otimes (V_p + \cdots + V_{-p})$. We must multiply $\sum_{s+t+u=l}(z^2)^s(z \cdot w)^t(w^2)^u$ to obtain polynomials in S_n. If we multiply $(z^2)^s(z \cdot w)^t(w^2)^u$ to an element of V_k, then it becomes a polynomial in

$V_{k+2s-2u}$. Hence the multiplicity of $(p\Lambda_1 + q\Lambda_2) \otimes V_k$ in S_n is equal to the coefficient of z^k in

$$(z^p + z^{p-2} + \cdots + z^{-p}) \sum_{s+t+u=l} z^{2s-2u} = (z^p + z^{p-2} + \cdots + z^{-p}) \sum_{s+u \leq l} z^{2s-2u}.$$

It is easy to see that this is equal to

$$\frac{(1 - z^{2l+2})(1 - z^{2l+4})(1 - z^{2p+2})}{z^{p+2l}(1 - z^2)^2(1 - z^4)},$$

which is the desired expression.

As is easily seen, the character of the principal part P_n just coincides with the decomposition formula of harmonic polynomials $\mathcal{H}_n$ for the part $p + 2q = n$ (cf. [11; Theorem 3.1]). Hence the principal part P_n is necessarily harmonic.

Remaining statements in Theorem 3.1 are easily verified. q.e.d.

Note that the multiplicity of $\mathcal{H}_n$ is at most 2, as stated in [11; p.127].

We can easily calculate the generating function of the principal part

$$P_n = \sum_{\substack{p+2q=n,\\p\geq 0, q\geq 0}} (p\Lambda_1 + q\Lambda_2) \otimes (V_p + V_{p-2} + \cdots + V_{-(p-2)} + V_{-p}).$$

In case $n \equiv 1 \pmod{2}$, it is equal to

$$\frac{x^{n+2} - xy^{(n+1)/2}z^{n+1}}{z^n(1 - z^2)(x^2 - yz^2)} - \frac{x^{n+2}z^{n+4} - xy^{(n+1)/2}z^3}{(1 - z^2)(x^2z^2 - y)},$$

and in case $n \equiv 0 \pmod{2}$, it is equal to

$$\frac{x^{n+2} - y^{(n+2)/2}z^{n+2}}{z^n(1 - z^2)(x^2 - yz^2)} - \frac{x^{n+2}z^{n+4} - y^{(n+2)/2}z^2}{(1 - z^2)(x^2z^2 - y)}.$$

The generating function of S_n is then obtained by multiplying the generating function of P_{n-2l} with the sum

$$\sum_{s+u \leq l} z^{2s-2u} = \frac{(1 - z^{2l+2})(1 - z^{2l+4})}{z^{2l}(1 - z^2)(1 - z^4)},$$

and add these products for $l = 0 \sim [n/2]$. Then in case $n \equiv 1 \pmod{2}$ it is equal to

$$\frac{xz^3(1 + z^2)}{(1 - y)(1 - z^2)^2(1 - x^2z^2)(x^2 - z^2)} + \frac{x^{n+8}z^{n+10}}{(1 - x^2)(1 - z^2)(1 - x^2z^2)(1 - x^2z^4)(x^2z^2 - y)}$$

$$+ \frac{xz^{-n}}{(1 - x^2)(1 - z^2)^2(1 - x^2z^4)(1 - yz^2)} - \frac{x^{n+8}z^{-n}}{(1 - x^2)(1 - z^2)(x^2 - z^2)(x^2 - z^4)(x^2 - yz^2)}$$

$$+ \frac{xz^{n+10}}{(1 - x^2)(1 - z^2)^2(x^2 - z^4)(y - z^2)} + \frac{xy^{(n+9)/2}z^3(1 + z^2)}{(1 - y)(1 - yz^2)(y - z^2)(x^2 - yz^2)(x^2z^2 - y)},$$

and in case $n \equiv 0 \pmod 2$ it is equal to

$$\frac{z^4(1+x^2)}{(1-y)(1-z^2)^2(1-x^2z^2)(x^2-z^2)} + \frac{x^{n+8}z^{n+10}}{(1-x^2)(1-z^2)(1-x^2z^2)(1-x^2z^4)(x^2z^2-y)}$$
$$+ \frac{z^{-n}(1+x^2z^2)}{(1-x^2)(1-z^2)(1-z^4)(1-x^2z^4)(1-yz^2)} - \frac{x^{n+8}z^{-n}}{(1-x^2)(1-z^2)(x^2-z^2)(x^2-z^4)(x^2-yz^2)}$$
$$+ \frac{z^{n+10}(x^2+z^2)}{(1-x^2)(1-z^2)(1-z^4)(x^2-z^4)(y-z^2)} + \frac{y^{(n+8)/2}z^4(x^2+y)}{(1-y)(1-yz^2)(y-z^2)(x^2-yz^2)(x^2z^2-y)}.$$

The above formula for the case $n \equiv 1 \pmod 4$ just coincides with the one given in [11; p.131].

Next, we calculate the generating function of $\sum_n S_n$ as

$$\sum_n (\text{generating function of } S_n) \times t^n.$$

Then, it takes the following quite simple form:

$$\frac{z^3}{(1-t^2)(1-z^2t^2)(z^2-t^2)(z-xt)(1-xzt)(1-yt^2)}$$
$$= \frac{1}{(1-t^2)(1-z^2t^2)(1-t^2/z^2)(1-xt/z)(1-xzt)(1-yt^2)}.$$

This formula indicates that the polynomial ring $\sum_n S_n$ is freely generated by six elements z^2, $z \cdot w$, w^2, $z \cdot \alpha$, $w \cdot \alpha$ and $(z \cdot \alpha)(w \cdot \beta) - (z \cdot \beta)(w \cdot \alpha)$.

4. An Algorithm to Obtain the Explicit Irreducible Decomposition

In this section we first give an algorithm to obtain the generator of each irreducible component of the space S_n. Concerning the space $\mathcal{H}_n$, we consider their generators in the latter part of this section.

By Theorem 3.1 the lower components of S_n can be obtained by multiplying the principal irreducible components of low degree and the product of three quadratic polynomials z^2, $z \cdot w$, w^2. Thus we first explain a method to obtain the generators of the principal irreducible components of P_n.

First, as stated before, S_n is a direct sum of the spaces of the form

$$T_{ab} U_{ab} = T_{ab} (V_{a-b} + V_{a-b-2} + \cdots + V_{-(a-b)}).$$

The symbol V_k implies that each monomial in the irreducible component $T_{ab}V_k$ is of the form $z_1^{c_1} \cdots z_p^{c_p} w_1^{d_1} \cdots w_p^{d_p}$ with $(c_1 + \cdots + c_p) - (d_1 + \cdots + d_p) = k$. The symbol T_{ab} implies that a generator of the $GL(p, \mathbf{C}) \times GL(2, \mathbf{C})$-irreducible component $T_{ab}U_{ab}$ is expressed as $x_1^{a-b}(x_1y_2 - x_2y_1)^b$ (see [1]). Since $z_j = x_j + iy_j$ and $w_j = x_j - iy_j$, we know that $x_1^{a-b}(x_1y_2 - x_2y_1)^b$ is equal to $(z_1 + w_1)^{a-b}(z_1w_2 - z_2w_1)^b$ up to a non-zero constant. Then to make a V_k-valued component, we must take a portion of the form $z_1^p w_1^q (z_1w_2 - z_2w_1)^b$ as a generator, where $p + q = a - b$ and $p - q = k$, i.e., $p = (a-b+k)/2$ and $q = (a-b-k)/2$. (Note that $|k| \leq a-b$ and $k \equiv a-b \pmod 2$. Hence both p and q are non-negative integers.)

For example, the $GL(p, \mathbf{C}) \times SO(2)$-irreducible component of the space $T_{52} V_1 \subset S_7$ is generated by the polynomial

$$z_1^2 w_1 (z_1 w_2 - z_2 w_1)^2.$$

In our notation, it can be represented as

$$(z \cdot \alpha)^2 (w \cdot \alpha) \{(z \cdot \alpha)(w \cdot \beta) - (z \cdot \beta)(w \cdot \alpha)\}^2$$

for some $\alpha, \beta \in \mathbf{C}^p$. The $GL(p, \mathbf{C})$-irreducible component T_{52} decomposes into the following eight $SO(p)$-irreducible factors:

$$(3\Lambda_1 + 2\Lambda_2) + (5\Lambda_1) + (3\Lambda_1 + \Lambda_2) + (\Lambda_1 + 2\Lambda_2) + 2(3\Lambda_1) + (\Lambda_1 + \Lambda_2) + (\Lambda_1).$$

(Here, the coefficient 2 of $(3\Lambda_1)$ indicates its multiplicity.) Hence we must impose some additional conditions on α and β to take out the principal $SO(p) \times SO(2)$-irreducible component $(3\Lambda_1 + 2\Lambda_2) \otimes V_1 \subset T_{52} V_1 \subset S_7$.

These conditions can be obtained from the orthogonality. The principal $SO(p) \times SO(2)$-irreducible component $(3\Lambda_1 + 2\Lambda_2) \otimes V_1$ must be orthogonal to the remaining seven components $(5\Lambda_1) \otimes V_1 \sim (\Lambda_1) \otimes V_1$ in $T_{52} V_1$, and by these orthogonality conditions, we can uniquely take out the desired $SO(p) \times SO(2)$-irreducible component $(3\Lambda_1 + 2\Lambda_2) \otimes V_1$. Actually, the component $(5\Lambda_1) \otimes V_1$ etc. appear in other terms $T_{ab} V_1$ in S_7, and they are also orthogonal to the principal component $(3\Lambda_1 + 2\Lambda_2) \otimes V_1$ since $T_{52} V_1$ and other $T_{ab} V_1$ are orthogonal in S_7. So we may impose orthogonality conditions to all irreducible components $(5\Lambda_1) \otimes V_1$ etc. in S_7. In this way, we can take out the generator of any principal irreducible component $(p\Lambda_1 + q\Lambda_2) \otimes V_k$ in S_{p+2q}.

As for the lower irreducible components, we can also obtain its generator by applying Theorem 3.1. In fact it is a product of the generator of a principal irreducible component for lower degree and a suitable product of three quadratic polynomials z^2, $z \cdot w$, w^2. In this way, we can obtain all generators of irreducible components of S_n explicitly.

Our remaining problem is to investigate the condition for the orthogonality. In the following, as one typical example, we explicitly solve this problem for the case S_5. General cases can be treated in the same way.

Remind that the $SO(p) \times SO(2)$-irreducible decomposition of S_5 is given by

$$\begin{aligned} S_5 &= T_5 U_5 + T_{41} U_{41} + T_{32} U_{32} \\ &= \{(5\Lambda_1) + (3\Lambda_1) + (\Lambda_1)\} \otimes (V_5 + V_3 + V_1 + V_{-1} + V_{-3} + V_{-5}) \\ &\quad + \{(3\Lambda_1 + \Lambda_2) + (3\Lambda_1) + (\Lambda_1 + \Lambda_2) + (\Lambda_1)\} \otimes (V_3 + V_1 + V_{-1} + V_{-3}) \\ &\quad + \{(\Lambda_1 + 2\Lambda_2) + (3\Lambda_1) + (\Lambda_1 + \Lambda_2) + (\Lambda_1)\} \otimes (V_1 + V_{-1}). \end{aligned}$$

Among them, the principal components are given by

$$\begin{aligned} P_5 &= (5\Lambda_1) \otimes (V_5 + V_3 + V_1 + V_{-1} + V_{-3} + V_{-5}) \\ &\quad + (3\Lambda_1 + \Lambda_2) \otimes (V_3 + V_1 + V_{-1} + V_{-3}) \\ &\quad + (\Lambda_1 + 2\Lambda_2) \otimes (V_1 + V_{-1}). \end{aligned}$$

Now we assume that the generator of each irreducible component of S_n for $n \leq 4$ is already known. (Its list will be given in §5.) Under this assumption, we obtain the generator of each component S_5. We first treat the cases of principal parts.

The generator of the irreducible component $(5\Lambda_1) \otimes V_5$ is expressed as $(z \cdot \alpha)^5$ for some $\alpha \in \mathbf{C}^p$. (We substitute $a = 5$, $b = 0$ and $k = 5$ into the expression $z_1^p w_1^q (z_1 w_2 - z_2 w_1)^b$, where $p = (a-b+k)/2$ and $q = (a-b-k)/2$. Then it becomes z_1^5, which corresponds to $(z \cdot \alpha)^5$.) This irreducible component must be orthogonal to the remaining components in $T_5 V_5$:

$$\{(3\Lambda_1) + (\Lambda_1)\} \otimes V_5.$$

These belong to the lower part of S_5. Hence they are products of the principal part of lower degree and three quadratic polynomials z^2, $z \cdot w$, w^2. The multiplicity of the component $(3\Lambda_1) \otimes V_5$ in S_5 is 1, and it is a product of the principal part $(3\Lambda_1) \otimes V_3 \subset S_3$ and $z^2 \in S_2$. (Note that if the term $(p\Lambda_1 + q\Lambda_2) \otimes V_k$ is the principal part, it must belong to S_{p+2q}.) The generator of the principal component $(3\Lambda_1) \otimes V_3$ of S_3 is given by $(z \cdot \beta)^3$, where $\beta \in \mathbf{C}^p$ with $\beta^2 = 0$. Thus to obtain the generator of $(5\Lambda_1) \otimes V_5$, we must impose the condition on α such that the inner product

$$\langle (z \cdot \alpha)^5, z^2 (z \cdot \beta)^3 \rangle = 0$$

for any $\beta \in \mathbf{C}^p$ with $\beta^2 = 0$. Similarly, the multiplicity of the component $(\Lambda_1) \otimes V_5$ in S_5 is 1, and it is a product of the principal part $(\Lambda_1) \otimes V_1 \subset S_1$ and $(z^2)^2 \in S_4$ in this case. Thus we must impose another condition on α

$$\langle (z \cdot \alpha)^5, (z^2)^2 (z \cdot \beta) \rangle = 0$$

for any $\beta \in \mathbf{C}^p$ with $\beta^2 = 0$.

In general th inner product $\langle z_1^{i_1} \cdots z_p^{i_p} w_1^{j_1} \cdots w_p^{j_p}, z_1^{k_1} \cdots z_p^{k_p} w_1^{l_1} \cdots w_p^{l_p} \rangle$ with $\sum i_u + \sum j_v = \sum k_u + \sum l_v$ is given by

$$\begin{cases} i_1! \cdots i_p! j_1! \cdots j_p! & (i_u = k_u, j_v = l_v, \forall u, v), \\ 0 & (\text{otherwise}). \end{cases}$$

By direct calculations we have

$$\begin{cases} \langle (z \cdot \alpha)^5, z^2 (z \cdot \beta)^3 \rangle = 120(\alpha^2)(\alpha \cdot \beta)^3, \\ \langle (z \cdot \alpha)^5, (z^2)^2 (z \cdot \beta) \rangle = 120(\alpha^2)^2 (\alpha \cdot \beta). \end{cases}$$

(Actually we use computers to calculate these inner products. See Conjecture 5.1 in §5.) We have $\alpha \cdot \beta \neq 0$ for generic β with $\beta^2 = 0$. Thus we must impose the condition $\alpha^2 = 0$ for the orthogonality condition. Hence, the generator of the principal irreducible component $(5\Lambda_1) \otimes V_5 \subset S_5$ is given by $(z \cdot \alpha)^5$ with $\alpha^2 = 0$.

Next, we consider the principal component $(5\Lambda_1) \otimes V_3$. In this case we have $a = 5$, $b = 0$ and $k = 3$ in the expression $z_1^p w_1^q (z_1 w_2 - z_2 w_1)^b$, where $p = (a-b+k)/2$ and $q = (a-b-k)/2$. Hence the candidate of the generator is $(z \cdot \alpha)^4 (w \cdot \alpha)$ in this case. The lower parts concerning this principal component are

$$\{(3\Lambda_1) + (\Lambda_1)\} \otimes V_3.$$

The multiplicities of these two components are both 2 in S_5. The components $(3\Lambda_1) \otimes V_k$ in S_3 are exhausted by

$$(3\Lambda_1) \otimes V_3, \quad (3\Lambda_1) \otimes V_1, \quad (3\Lambda_1) \otimes V_{-1}, \quad (3\Lambda_1) \otimes V_{-3},$$

and hence two components of $(3\Lambda_1) \otimes V_3$ are generated by

$$\begin{cases} (3\Lambda_1) \otimes V_3 \times (0) \otimes V_0, \\ (3\Lambda_1) \otimes V_1 \times (0) \otimes V_2, \end{cases}$$

which respectively correspond to $(z \cdot w)(z \cdot \beta)^3$ and $z^2(z \cdot \beta)^2(w \cdot \beta)$ with $\beta^2 = 0$ for both cases.

The components $(\Lambda_1) \otimes V_k$ in S_1 are exhausted by

$$(\Lambda_1) \otimes V_1, \quad (\Lambda_1) \otimes V_{-1},$$

and hence two components of $(\Lambda_1) \otimes V_3$ are generated by

$$\begin{cases} (\Lambda_1) \otimes V_1 \times (0) \otimes V_2, \\ (\Lambda_1) \otimes V_{-1} \times (0) \otimes V_4, \end{cases}$$

which respectively correspond to $z^2(z \cdot w)(z \cdot \beta)$ and $(z^2)^2(w \cdot \beta)$ with $\beta^2 = 0$. Note that z^2 is a generator of $(0) \otimes V_2$ and $z \cdot w$ is a generator of $(0) \otimes V_0$. Thus the product $z^2(z \cdot w)$ is a generator of $(0) \otimes V_2$ in S_4. Next, we calculate the inner products. The results are given by

$$\langle (z \cdot \alpha)^4(w \cdot \alpha), (z \cdot w)(z \cdot \beta)^3 \rangle = 24\alpha^2(\alpha \cdot \beta)^3,$$
$$\langle (z \cdot \alpha)^4(w \cdot \alpha), z^2(z \cdot \beta)^2(w \cdot \beta) \rangle = 24\alpha^2(\alpha \cdot \beta)^3,$$
$$\langle (z \cdot \alpha)^4(w \cdot \alpha), z^2(z \cdot w)(z \cdot \beta) \rangle = 24(\alpha^2)^2(\alpha \cdot \beta),$$
$$\langle (z \cdot \alpha)^4(w \cdot \alpha), (z^2)^2(w \cdot \beta) \rangle = 24(\alpha^2)^2(\alpha \cdot \beta).$$

(Here, we once use computers for the calculations.) Thus, by the same reason as above, we must impose the condition $\alpha^2 = 0$ to obtain the generator of the irreducible component. Hence the generator of the principal irreducible component $(5\Lambda_1) \otimes V_3$ in S_5 is given by $(z \cdot \alpha)^4(w \cdot \alpha)$ with $\alpha^2 = 0$.

Next, we consider the principal component $(5\Lambda_1) \otimes V_1$. We can obtain the generator of this component completely in the same way as above, and it is given by $(z \cdot \alpha)^3(w \cdot \alpha)^2$ with $\alpha^2 = 0$. We must calculate the inner products to obtain this final expression. The inner products are given as follows:

$$\langle (z \cdot \alpha)^3(w \cdot \alpha)^2, w^2(z \cdot \beta)^3 \rangle = 12\alpha^2(\alpha \cdot \beta)^3,$$
$$\langle (z \cdot \alpha)^3(w \cdot \alpha)^2, (z \cdot w)(z \cdot \beta)^2(w \cdot \beta) \rangle = 12\alpha^2(\alpha \cdot \beta)^3,$$
$$\langle (z \cdot \alpha)^3(w \cdot \alpha)^2, z^2(z \cdot \beta)(w \cdot \beta)^2 \rangle = 12\alpha^2(\alpha \cdot \beta)^3,$$
$$\langle (z \cdot \alpha)^3(w \cdot \alpha)^2, z^2 w^2(z \cdot \beta) \rangle = 12(\alpha^2)^2(\alpha \cdot \beta),$$
$$\langle (z \cdot \alpha)^3(w \cdot \alpha)^2, (z \cdot w)^2(z \cdot \beta) \rangle = 12(\alpha^2)^2(\alpha \cdot \beta),$$
$$\langle (z \cdot \alpha)^3(w \cdot \alpha)^2, z^2(z \cdot w)(w \cdot \beta) \rangle = 12(\alpha^2)^2(\alpha \cdot \beta).$$

We once use computers. The generators of $(5\Lambda_1) \otimes V_k$ for $k = -1, -3, -5$ are similarly obtained.

Next, we consider the principal components in $T_{41} U_{41} \subset S_5$:

$$T_{41} U_{41} = \{(3\Lambda_1 + \Lambda_2) + (3\Lambda_1) + (\Lambda_1 + \Lambda_2) + (\Lambda_1)\} \otimes (V_3 + V_1 + V_{-1} + V_{-3}).$$

We first treat the case $(3\Lambda_1 + \Lambda_2) \otimes V_3$. In this case, since $a = 4$, $b = 1$ and $k = 3$ in the expression $z_1^p w_1^q (z_1 w_2 - z_2 w_1)^b$, with $p = (a - b + k)/2$ and $q = (a - b - k)/2$, the candidate of the generator is $z_1^3 (z_1 w_2 - z_2 w_1)$, which is equivalent to $(z \cdot \alpha)^3 \{(z \cdot \alpha)(w \cdot \beta) - (z \cdot \beta)(w \cdot \alpha)\}$ in our notation. Then we must find conditions on α and β such that it is orthogonal to

$$\{(3\Lambda_1) + (\Lambda_1 + \Lambda_2) + (\Lambda_1)\} \otimes V_3.$$

As we have already seen, the multiplicity of $(3\Lambda_1) \otimes V_3$ in S_5 is 2 and we express their generators as $(z \cdot w)(z \cdot \gamma)^3$, $z^2 (z \cdot \gamma)^2 (w \cdot \gamma)$ with $\gamma^2 = 0$ in this case. The multiplicity of $(\Lambda_1 + \Lambda_2) \otimes V_3$ in S_5 is 1. In S_3 the irreducible components of the form $(\Lambda_1 + \Lambda_2) \otimes V_k$ are exhausted by

$$(\Lambda_1 + \Lambda_2) \otimes V_1, \qquad (\Lambda_1 + \Lambda_2) \otimes V_{-1}.$$

Hence the irreducible component is a product of $(\Lambda_1 + \Lambda_2) \otimes V_1$ and z^2, i.e., its generator is given by $z^2 (z \cdot \gamma)\{(z \cdot \gamma)(w \cdot \delta) - (z \cdot \delta)(w \cdot \gamma)\}$ with $\gamma^2 = \gamma \cdot \delta = \delta^2 = 0$. The generators of $(\Lambda_1) \otimes V_3$ are $z^2 (z \cdot w)(z \cdot \gamma)$ and $(z^2)^2 (w \cdot \gamma)$ with $\gamma^2 = 0$, as we already verified.

As for the inner products with $\varphi = (z \cdot \alpha)^3 \{(z \cdot \alpha)(w \cdot \beta) - (z \cdot \beta)(w \cdot \alpha)\}$, we can calculate them by using computers. Their results are given by

$$\langle \varphi, (z \cdot w)(z \cdot \gamma)^3 \rangle = 18(\alpha \cdot \gamma)^2 \{(\alpha \cdot \beta)(\alpha \cdot \gamma) - \alpha^2 (\beta \cdot \gamma)\},$$
$$\langle \varphi, z^2 (z \cdot \gamma)^2 (w \cdot \gamma) \rangle = -12(\alpha \cdot \gamma)^2 \{(\alpha \cdot \beta)(\alpha \cdot \gamma) - \alpha^2 (\beta \cdot \gamma)\},$$
$$\langle \varphi, z^2 (z \cdot \gamma)\{(z \cdot \gamma)(w \cdot \delta) - (z \cdot \delta)(w \cdot \gamma)\}\rangle$$
$$= 30\alpha^2 (\alpha \cdot \gamma)\{(\alpha \cdot \gamma)(\beta \cdot \delta) - (\alpha \cdot \delta)(\beta \cdot \gamma)\},$$
$$\langle \varphi, z^2 (z \cdot w)(z \cdot \gamma) \rangle = 6\alpha^2 \{(\alpha \cdot \beta)(\alpha \cdot \gamma) - \alpha^2 (\beta \cdot \gamma)\},$$
$$\langle \varphi, (z^2)^2 (w \cdot \gamma) \rangle = -24\alpha^2 \{(\alpha \cdot \beta)(\alpha \cdot \gamma) - \alpha^2 (\beta \cdot \gamma)\}.$$

We have $\alpha \cdot \gamma \neq 0$ for generic γ with $\gamma^2 = 0$. Hence the equality $(\alpha \cdot \beta)(\alpha \cdot \gamma) - \alpha^2 (\beta \cdot \gamma) = 0$ must be hold. Since γ is generic with $\gamma^2 = 0$, we have $(\alpha \cdot \beta)\alpha - \alpha^2 \beta = 0$. If $\alpha \cdot \beta \neq 0$, then α is parallel to β, and hence $\varphi = 0$. This contradicts to the fact that φ is a generator of the irreducible component. Hence we have $\alpha \cdot \beta = 0$, and consequently $\alpha^2 \beta = 0$. If $\beta = 0$, then we have $\varphi = 0$, which is a contradiction. Hence we have $\alpha^2 = 0$.

Therefore, the generator of the principal irreducible component $(3\Lambda_1 + \Lambda_2) \otimes V_3$ in S_5 is given by $(z \cdot \alpha)^3 \{(z \cdot \alpha)(w \cdot \beta) - (z \cdot \beta)(w \cdot \alpha)\}$ with $\alpha^2 = \alpha \cdot \beta = 0$. Clearly we may impose the additional condition $\beta^2 = 0$, since it also gives a non-zero element in the irreducible component.

Next, we consider the component $(3\Lambda_1 + \Lambda_2) \otimes V_1$. As before, we can obtain the candidate of the generator of this component, which is given by

$$(z \cdot \alpha)^2 (w \cdot \alpha)\{(z \cdot \alpha)(w \cdot \beta) - (z \cdot \beta)(w \cdot \alpha)\}.$$

The orthogonality conditions to the lower components
$$\{(3\Lambda_1) + (\Lambda_1 + \Lambda_2) + (\Lambda_1)\} \otimes V_1$$
are obtained by the following way: The multiplicities of three irreducible components of $(3\Lambda_1) \otimes V_1$, $(\Lambda_1 + \Lambda_2) \otimes V_1$ and $(\Lambda_1) \otimes V_1$ are respectively 3, 2 and 3 in S_5, and their generators are given by

- $w^2(z \cdot \gamma)^3$, $(z \cdot w)(z \cdot \gamma)^2(w \cdot \gamma)$, $z^2(z \cdot \gamma)(w \cdot \gamma)^2$,
- $(z \cdot w)(z \cdot \gamma)\{(z \cdot \gamma)(w \cdot \delta) - (z \cdot \delta)(w \cdot \gamma)\}$,
  $$z^2(w \cdot \gamma)\{(z \cdot \gamma)(w \cdot \delta) - (z \cdot \delta)(w \cdot \gamma)\},$$
- $(z \cdot w)^2(z \cdot \gamma)$, $z^2 w^2(z \cdot \gamma)$, $z^2(z \cdot w)(w \cdot \gamma)$,

with $\gamma^2 = \gamma \cdot \delta = \delta^2 = 0$, respectively. We calculate the inner products with the generator $(z \cdot \alpha)^2(w \cdot \alpha)\{(z \cdot \alpha)(w \cdot \beta) - (z \cdot \beta)(w \cdot \alpha)\}$. The results are given by

- $12(\alpha \cdot \gamma)^2 A$, $2(\alpha \cdot \gamma)^2 A$, $-8(\alpha \cdot \gamma)^2 A$,
- $10\alpha^2(\alpha \cdot \gamma)B$, $10\alpha^2(\alpha \cdot \gamma)B$,
- $4\alpha^2 A$, $4\alpha^2 A$, $-6\alpha^2 A$,

where $A = (\alpha \cdot \beta)(\alpha \cdot \gamma) - \alpha^2(\beta \cdot \gamma)$ and $B = (\alpha \cdot \gamma)(\beta \cdot \delta) - (\alpha \cdot \delta)(\beta \cdot \gamma)$. Then, as above, we have two conditions $\alpha^2 = \alpha \cdot \beta = 0$ to insure the orthogonality, and we may also impose the additional condition $\beta^2 = 0$.

The generators of the remaining components $(3\Lambda_1 + \Lambda_2) \otimes V_{-1}$ and $(3\Lambda_1 + \Lambda_2) \otimes V_{-3}$ are similarly obtained.

Finally, we consider the principal components in $T_{32} U_{32}$:
$$T_{32} U_{32} = \{(\Lambda_1 + 2\Lambda_2) + (3\Lambda_1) + (\Lambda_1 + \Lambda_2) + (\Lambda_1)\} \otimes (V_1 + V_{-1}).$$

As for the principal component $(\Lambda_1 + 2\Lambda_2) \otimes V_1$, we have $a = 3$, $b = 2$ and $k = 1$ in the expression $z_1^p w_1^q(z_1 w_2 - z_2 w_1)^b$, where $p = (a-b+k)/2 = 1$ and $q = (a-b-k)/2 = 0$. Hence the candidate of the generator is $z_1(z_1 w_2 - z_2 w_1)^2$, which is equivalent to $(z \cdot \alpha)\{(z \cdot \alpha)(w \cdot \beta) - (z \cdot \beta)(w \cdot \alpha)\}^2$. Then we must find conditions on α and β such that it is orthogonal to
$$\{(3\Lambda_1) + (\Lambda_1 + \Lambda_2) + (\Lambda_1)\} \otimes V_1.$$
These components are those which we just computed above.

Using the same generators again, we compute the inner products with the generator $(z \cdot \alpha)\{(z \cdot \alpha)(w \cdot \beta) - (z \cdot \beta)(w \cdot \alpha)\}^2$. Their results are given by

- $12(\alpha \cdot \gamma)C$, $-4(\alpha \cdot \gamma)C$, $4(\alpha \cdot \gamma)C$,
- $8D$, $-16D$,
- $-8(\alpha \cdot \gamma)E$, $16(\alpha \cdot \gamma)E$, 0,

where
$$C = \alpha^2(\beta \cdot \gamma)^2 - 2(\alpha \cdot \beta)(\beta \cdot \gamma)(\gamma \cdot \alpha) + \beta^2(\alpha \cdot \gamma)^2,$$
$$D = \{(\alpha \cdot \gamma)(\beta \cdot \delta) - (\alpha \cdot \delta)(\beta \cdot \gamma)\}\{(\alpha \cdot \beta)(\alpha \cdot \gamma) - \alpha^2(\beta \cdot \gamma)\},$$
$$E = \alpha^2 \beta^2 - (\alpha \cdot \beta)^2.$$

We have $(\alpha\cdot\gamma)(\beta\cdot\delta)-(\alpha\cdot\delta)(\beta\cdot\gamma)\neq 0$ for generic γ, δ with $\gamma^2=\gamma\cdot\delta=\delta^2=0$. Hence we have $(\alpha\cdot\beta)(\alpha\cdot\gamma)-\alpha^2(\beta\cdot\gamma)=0$, and from this condition we have $\alpha^2=\alpha\cdot\beta=0$, in the same way as before. Then, from the condition $C=0$, we have $\beta^2=0$, since $\alpha\cdot\gamma\neq 0$ for generic γ wirh $\gamma^2=0$. Therefore, the generator of the principal component $(\Lambda_1+2\Lambda_2)\otimes V_1$ is given by $(z\cdot\alpha)\{(z\cdot\alpha)(w\cdot\beta)-(z\cdot\beta)(w\cdot\alpha)\}^2$ with $\alpha^2=\alpha\cdot\beta=\beta^2=0$. The generator of $(\Lambda_1+2\Lambda_2)\otimes V_{-1}$ is similarly obtained.

Thus, we obtained the generators of all principal components of S_5. Lower components of S_5 are already obtained from the assumption that the generators of S_n for $n\leq 4$ is known. We have only to multiply three quadratic polynomials z^2, $z\cdot w$, w^2 to these generators to obtain generators of lower components with degree 5 (cf. Theorem 3.1).

Next we consider the space of harmonic polynomials $\mathcal{H}_n$. As for the principal components, $SO(p)\times SO(2)$-irreducible decompositions for both spaces S_n and $\mathcal{H}_n$ coincide, and this case is just completed.

In the following, we consider the lower components. For each type of $SO(p)\times SO(2)$-irreducible component of S_n, we first count its multiplicity. If the multiplicity is 1, we have only to determine whether it is harmonic or not. If the multiplicity is greater than 1, then we make a linear combination of these generators, and find a condition on coefficients so that it is harmonic.

In the following, we carry out this procedure for the lower components of S_5, as one typical example.

First, the multiplicity of the following irreducible components of S_5 and $\mathcal{H}_5$ coincide, and hence they are automatically harmonic:

$$(3\Lambda_1)\otimes V_5,\quad (3\Lambda_1)\otimes V_{-5},\quad (\Lambda_1+\Lambda_2)\otimes V_3,\quad (\Lambda_1+\Lambda_2)\otimes V_{-3},$$
$$(\Lambda_1)\otimes V_5,\quad (\Lambda_1)\otimes V_{-5}.$$

Next, we consider the component $(3\Lambda_1)\otimes V_3$. As we stated before, the multiplicity of this space is 2, and they are generated by $(z\cdot w)(z\cdot\alpha)^3$ and $z^2(z\cdot\alpha)^2(w\cdot\alpha)$ with $\alpha^2=0$. We remind that the function $f(z_1,\cdots,z_p,w_1,\cdots,w_p)$ is harmonic if and only if

$$\sum_i \frac{\partial^2 f}{\partial z_i \partial w_i}=0,\qquad \sum_{i,j}\frac{\partial^2}{\partial z_i^2}\left(\frac{\partial^2 f}{\partial w_j^2}\right)=0.$$

In this case the second condition is automatically satisfied, since both generators are linear with respect to w_i. As for the first condition, we have

$$\sum_i \frac{\partial^2}{\partial z_i \partial w_i}(z\cdot w)(z\cdot\alpha)^3=(p+3)(z\cdot\alpha)^3,$$

$$\sum_i \frac{\partial^2}{\partial z_i \partial w_i}z^2(z\cdot\alpha)^2(w\cdot\alpha)=2(z\cdot\alpha)^3,$$

because $\alpha^2=0$. Thus the harmonic component is generated by

$$(p+3)\,z^2(z\cdot\alpha)^2(w\cdot\alpha)-2(z\cdot w)(z\cdot\alpha)^3$$

in this case. The harmonic component $(3\Lambda_1)\otimes V_{-3}$ is similarly obtained.

Next we consider the case $(3\Lambda_1) \otimes V_1$. The multiplicity of this space in S_5 is 3, and these spaces are generated by

$$w^2(z \cdot \alpha)^3, \quad (z \cdot w)(z \cdot \alpha)^2(w \cdot \alpha), \quad z^2(z \cdot \alpha)(w \cdot \alpha)^2,$$

as we stated before. We calculate their derivatives. As for the first derivative, we have

$$\sum_i \frac{\partial^2}{\partial z_i \partial w_i} w^2(z \cdot \alpha)^3 = 6(z \cdot \alpha)^2(w \cdot \alpha),$$

$$\sum_i \frac{\partial^2}{\partial z_i \partial w_i} (z \cdot w)(z \cdot \alpha)^2(w \cdot \alpha) = (p+3)\,(z \cdot \alpha)^2(w \cdot \alpha),$$

$$\sum_i \frac{\partial^2}{\partial z_i \partial w_i} z^2(z \cdot \alpha)(w \cdot \alpha)^2 = 4(z \cdot \alpha)^2(w \cdot \alpha).$$

Here, we once use the assumption $\alpha^2 = 0$. Concerning the second derivative, we have

$$\sum_i \frac{\partial^2}{\partial z_i^2} w^2(z \cdot \alpha)^3 = 0,$$

$$\sum_i \frac{\partial^2}{\partial z_i^2} (z \cdot w)(z \cdot \alpha)^2(w \cdot \alpha) = 4(z \cdot \alpha)(w \cdot \alpha)^2,$$

$$\sum_j \frac{\partial^2}{\partial w_j^2} 4(z \cdot \alpha)(w \cdot \alpha)^2 = 0,$$

$$\sum_i \frac{\partial^2}{\partial z_i^2} z^2(z \cdot \alpha)(w \cdot \alpha)^2 = (2p+4)\,(z \cdot \alpha)(w \cdot \alpha)^2,$$

$$\sum_j \frac{\partial^2}{\partial w_j^2} (2p+4)\,(z \cdot \alpha)(w \cdot \alpha)^2 = 2(2p+4)\,(z \cdot \alpha)\alpha^2 = 0.$$

Thus we have $\sum_{i,j} \frac{\partial^2}{\partial z_i^2} \left(\frac{\partial^2 f}{\partial w_j^2} \right) = 0$ for $f = w^2(z \cdot \alpha)^3$, $(z \cdot w)(z \cdot \alpha)^2(w \cdot \alpha)$ and $z^2(z \cdot \alpha)(w \cdot \alpha)^2$. Hence two irreducible harmonic components are generated by

$$(p+3)z^2(z \cdot \alpha)(w \cdot \alpha)^2 - 4(z \cdot w)(z \cdot \alpha)^2(w \cdot \alpha),$$
$$3z^2(z \cdot \alpha)(w \cdot \alpha)^2 - 2w^2(z \cdot \alpha)^3,$$

respectively. The harmonic components $(3\Lambda_1) \otimes V_{-1}$ are similarly obtained.

Next, we consider the case $(\Lambda_1 + \Lambda_2) \otimes V_1$. In this case the multiplicity in S_5 is 2, and the irreducible components are generated by

$$f = (z \cdot w)(z \cdot \alpha)\{(z \cdot \alpha)(w \cdot \beta) - (z \cdot \beta)(w \cdot \alpha)\},$$
$$g = z^2(w \cdot \alpha)\{(z \cdot \alpha)(w \cdot \beta) - (z \cdot \beta)(w \cdot \alpha)\}.$$

Then we have

$$\sum_i \frac{\partial^2 f}{\partial z_i \partial w_i} = (p+3)(z\cdot\alpha)\{(z\cdot\alpha)(w\cdot\beta) - (z\cdot\beta)(w\cdot\alpha)\},$$

$$\sum_i \frac{\partial^2 g}{\partial z_i \partial w_i} = 2(z\cdot\alpha)\{(z\cdot\alpha)(w\cdot\beta) - (z\cdot\beta)(w\cdot\alpha)\}.$$

Concerning the second derivative, we have

$$\sum_j \frac{\partial^2 f}{\partial w_j^2} = \sum_j \frac{\partial^2 g}{\partial w_j^2} = 0.$$

(In these calculations, we used the property $\alpha^2 = \alpha\cdot\beta = 0$.) Thus the harmonic component is generated by $(p+3)g - 2f$. The harmonic component of $(\Lambda_1 + \Lambda_2) \otimes V_{-1}$ is similarly obtained.

For the remaining case $(\Lambda_1) \otimes V_3$, by the same method, we can obtain the harmonic component. After some calculations, we know that it is generated by

$$(p+3)(z^2)^2(w\cdot\alpha) - 4z^2(z\cdot w)(z\cdot\alpha).$$

The case $(\Lambda_1) \otimes V_{-3}$ can be treated in the same way.

5. Tables of Generators of S_n and $\mathcal{H}_n$ for $n \leq 5$

We here give tables of the multiplicities and generators of all irreducible components of the spaces S_n and $\mathcal{H}_n$ for the cases $n \leq 5$ as a reference. Remark that the dimension of the $SO(p) \times SO(2)$-irreducible component $(r\Lambda_1 + s\Lambda_2) \otimes V_k$ can be calculated by the formula

$$\frac{1}{(p-2)!(p-4)!}(r+1)(2s+p-4)(r+2s+p-3)$$
$$\times (2r+2s+p-2) \cdot \prod_{l=1}^{p-5}(s+l) \cdot \prod_{l=2}^{p-4}(r+s+l).$$

In the following we assume $\alpha^2 = \alpha\cdot\beta = \beta^2 = 0$. The coefficient of $(p\Lambda_1 + q\Lambda_2) \otimes V_k$ implies its multiplicity.

Table of S_n for $n \leq 5$:

S_1: principal components
    $(\Lambda_1) \otimes V_1 : (z\cdot\alpha),$
    $(\Lambda_1) \otimes V_{-1} : (w\cdot\alpha).$

S_2: principal components
    $(2\Lambda_1) \otimes V_2 : (z\cdot\alpha)^2,$
    $(2\Lambda_1) \otimes V_0 : (z\cdot\alpha)(w\cdot\alpha),$
    $(2\Lambda_1) \otimes V_{-2} : (w\cdot\alpha)^2,$
    $(\Lambda_2) \otimes V_0 : (z\cdot\alpha)(w\cdot\beta) - (z\cdot\beta)(w\cdot\alpha).$

lower components
$(0) \otimes V_2 : z^2,$
$(0) \otimes V_0 : z \cdot w,$
$(0) \otimes V_{-2} : w^2.$

S_3: principal components
$(3\Lambda_1) \otimes V_3 : (z \cdot \alpha)^3,$
$(3\Lambda_1) \otimes V_1 : (z \cdot \alpha)^2 (w \cdot \alpha),$
$(3\Lambda_1) \otimes V_{-1} : (z \cdot \alpha)(w \cdot \alpha)^2,$
$(3\Lambda_1) \otimes V_{-3} : (w \cdot \alpha)^3,$
$(\Lambda_1 + \Lambda_2) \otimes V_1 : (z \cdot \alpha)\{(z \cdot \alpha)(w \cdot \beta) - (z \cdot \beta)(w \cdot \alpha)\},$
$(\Lambda_1 + \Lambda_2) \otimes V_{-1} : (w \cdot \alpha)\{(z \cdot \alpha)(w \cdot \beta) - (z \cdot \beta)(w \cdot \alpha)\}.$

lower components
$(\Lambda_1) \otimes V_3 : z^2(z \cdot \alpha),$
$2(\Lambda_1) \otimes V_1 : z^2(w \cdot \alpha), \quad (z \cdot w)(z \cdot \alpha),$
$2(\Lambda_1) \otimes V_{-1} : (z \cdot w)(w \cdot \alpha), \quad w^2(z \cdot \alpha),$
$(\Lambda_1) \otimes V_{-3} : w^2(w \cdot \alpha).$

S_4: principal components
$(4\Lambda_1) \otimes V_4 : (z \cdot \alpha)^4,$
$(4\Lambda_1) \otimes V_2 : (z \cdot \alpha)^3(w \cdot \alpha),$
$(4\Lambda_1) \otimes V_0 : (z \cdot \alpha)^2(w \cdot \alpha)^2,$
$(4\Lambda_1) \otimes V_{-2} : (z \cdot \alpha)(w \cdot \alpha)^3,$
$(4\Lambda_1) \otimes V_{-4} : (w \cdot \alpha)^4,$
$(2\Lambda_1 + \Lambda_2) \otimes V_2 : (z \cdot \alpha)^2\{(z \cdot \alpha)(w \cdot \beta) - (z \cdot \beta)(w \cdot \alpha)\},$
$(2\Lambda_1 + \Lambda_2) \otimes V_0 : (z \cdot \alpha)(w \cdot \alpha)\{(z \cdot \alpha)(w \cdot \beta) - (z \cdot \beta)(w \cdot \alpha)\},$
$(2\Lambda_1 + \Lambda_2) \otimes V_{-2} : (w \cdot \alpha)^2\{(z \cdot \alpha)(w \cdot \beta) - (z \cdot \beta)(w \cdot \alpha)\},$
$(2\Lambda_2) \otimes V_0 : \{(z \cdot \alpha)(w \cdot \beta) - (z \cdot \beta)(w \cdot \alpha)\}^2.$

lower components
$(2\Lambda_1) \otimes V_4 : z^2(z \cdot \alpha)^2,$
$2(2\Lambda_1) \otimes V_2 : z^2(z \cdot \alpha)(w \cdot \alpha), \quad (z \cdot w)(z \cdot \alpha)^2,$
$3(2\Lambda_1) \otimes V_0 : z^2(w \cdot \alpha)^2, \quad (z \cdot w)(z \cdot \alpha)(w \cdot \alpha), \quad w^2(z \cdot \alpha)^2,$
$2(2\Lambda_1) \otimes V_{-2} : (z \cdot w)(w \cdot \alpha)^2, \quad w^2(z \cdot \alpha)(w \cdot \alpha),$
$(2\Lambda_1) \otimes V_{-4} : w^2(w \cdot \alpha)^2,$
$(\Lambda_2) \otimes V_2 : z^2\{(z \cdot \alpha)(w \cdot \beta) - (z \cdot \beta)(w \cdot \alpha)\},$
$(\Lambda_2) \otimes V_0 : (z \cdot w)\{(z \cdot \alpha)(w \cdot \beta) - (z \cdot \beta)(w \cdot \alpha)\},$
$(\Lambda_2) \otimes V_{-2} : w^2\{(z \cdot \alpha)(w \cdot \beta) - (z \cdot \beta)(w \cdot \alpha)\},$
$(0) \otimes V_4 : (z^2)^2,$
$(0) \otimes V_2 : z^2(z \cdot w),$
$2(0) \otimes V_0 : z^2 w^2, \quad (z \cdot w)^2,$
$(0) \otimes V_{-2} : w^2(z \cdot w),$
$(0) \otimes V_{-4} : (w^2)^2.$

S_5: principal components
$(5\Lambda_1) \otimes V_5 : (z \cdot \alpha)^5,$
$(5\Lambda_1) \otimes V_3 : (z \cdot \alpha)^4(w \cdot \alpha),$
$(5\Lambda_1) \otimes V_1 : (z \cdot \alpha)^3(w \cdot \alpha)^2,$
$(5\Lambda_1) \otimes V_{-1} : (z \cdot \alpha)^2(w \cdot \alpha)^3,$

$(5\Lambda_1) \otimes V_{-3} : (z \cdot \alpha)(w \cdot \alpha)^4,$
$(5\Lambda_1) \otimes V_{-5} : (w \cdot \alpha)^5,$
$(3\Lambda_1 + \Lambda_2) \otimes V_3 : (z \cdot \alpha)^3 \{(z \cdot \alpha)(w \cdot \beta) - (z \cdot \beta)(w \cdot \alpha)\},$
$(3\Lambda_1 + \Lambda_2) \otimes V_1 : (z \cdot \alpha)^2 (w \cdot \alpha) \{(z \cdot \alpha)(w \cdot \beta) - (z \cdot \beta)(w \cdot \alpha)\},$
$(3\Lambda_1 + \Lambda_2) \otimes V_{-1} : (z \cdot \alpha)(w \cdot \alpha)^2 \{(z \cdot \alpha)(w \cdot \beta) - (z \cdot \beta)(w \cdot \alpha)\},$
$(3\Lambda_1 + \Lambda_2) \otimes V_{-3} : (w \cdot \alpha)^3 \{(z \cdot \alpha)(w \cdot \beta) - (z \cdot \beta)(w \cdot \alpha)\},$
$(\Lambda_1 + 2\Lambda_2) \otimes V_1 : (z \cdot \alpha)\{(z \cdot \alpha)(w \cdot \beta) - (z \cdot \beta)(w \cdot \alpha)\}^2,$
$(\Lambda_1 + 2\Lambda_2) \otimes V_{-1} : (w \cdot \alpha)\{(z \cdot \alpha)(w \cdot \beta) - (z \cdot \beta)(w \cdot \alpha)\}^2.$

lower components

$(3\Lambda_1) \otimes V_5 : z^2(z \cdot \alpha)^3,$
$2(3\Lambda_1) \otimes V_3 : z^2(z \cdot \alpha)^2(w \cdot \alpha), \quad (z \cdot w)(z \cdot \alpha)^3,$
$3(3\Lambda_1) \otimes V_1 : z^2(z \cdot \alpha)(w \cdot \alpha)^2, \quad (z \cdot w)(z \cdot \alpha)^2(w \cdot \alpha), \quad w^2(z \cdot \alpha)^3,$
$3(3\Lambda_1) \otimes V_{-1} : z^2(w \cdot \alpha)^3, \quad (z \cdot w)(z \cdot \alpha)(w \cdot \alpha)^2, \quad w^2(z \cdot \alpha)^2(w \cdot \alpha),$
$2(3\Lambda_1) \otimes V_{-3} : (z \cdot w)(w \cdot \alpha)^3, \quad w^2(z \cdot \alpha)(w \cdot \alpha)^2,$
$(3\Lambda_1) \otimes V_{-5} : w^2(w \cdot \alpha)^3,$
$(\Lambda_1 + \Lambda_2) \otimes V_3 : z^2(z \cdot \alpha)\{(z \cdot \alpha)(w \cdot \beta) - (z \cdot \beta)(w \cdot \alpha)\},$
$2(\Lambda_1 + \Lambda_2) \otimes V_1 : z^2(w \cdot \alpha)\{(z \cdot \alpha)(w \cdot \beta) - (z \cdot \beta)(w \cdot \alpha)\},$
$\qquad (z \cdot w)(z \cdot \alpha)\{(z \cdot \alpha)(w \cdot \beta) - (z \cdot \beta)(w \cdot \alpha)\},$
$2(\Lambda_1 + \Lambda_2) \otimes V_{-1} : (z \cdot w)(w \cdot \alpha)\{(z \cdot \alpha)(w \cdot \beta) - (z \cdot \beta)(w \cdot \alpha)\},$
$\qquad w^2(z \cdot \alpha)\{(z \cdot \alpha)(w \cdot \beta) - (z \cdot \beta)(w \cdot \alpha)\},$
$(\Lambda_1 + \Lambda_2) \otimes V_{-3} : w^2(w \cdot \alpha)\{(z \cdot \alpha)(w \cdot \beta) - (z \cdot \beta)(w \cdot \alpha)\},$
$(\Lambda_1) \otimes V_5 : (z^2)^2(z \cdot \alpha),$
$2(\Lambda_1) \otimes V_3 : (z^2)^2(w \cdot \alpha), \quad z^2(z \cdot w)(z \cdot \alpha),$
$3(\Lambda_1) \otimes V_1 : z^2(z \cdot w)(w \cdot \alpha), \quad z^2 w^2(z \cdot \alpha), \quad (z \cdot w)^2(z \cdot \alpha),$
$3(\Lambda_1) \otimes V_{-1} : z^2 w^2(w \cdot \alpha), \quad (z \cdot w)^2(w \cdot \alpha), \quad w^2(z \cdot w)(z \cdot \alpha),$
$2(\Lambda_1) \otimes V_{-3} : w^2(z \cdot w)(w \cdot \alpha), \quad (w^2)^2(z \cdot \alpha),$
$(\Lambda_1) \otimes V_{-5} : (w^2)^2(w \cdot \alpha).$

The generators of principal components of S_n for general n can be easily observed by these data. But to verify it, we must calculate the inner products of several generators. As we have seen before, the inner products take several complicated forms concerning α and β and it is hard to obtain their general formulas at present. We give here one conjecture on the inner product, concerning only on the variable z:

Conjecture 5.1. *Assume* $2k + l = 2m + n$. *Then we have*

$$\langle (z^2)^k (z \cdot \alpha)^l, (z^2)^m (z \cdot \beta)^n \rangle =$$
$$\sum_s \frac{k!\, l!\, m!\, n!\, 2^s}{(k-s)!\, (m-s)!\, (2s+l-2m)!\, s!} \prod_{t=0}^{s-1} (p + 2k + 2l - 2m + 2t)$$
$$\times (\alpha^2)^{m-s} (\beta^2)^{k-s} (\alpha \cdot \beta)^{2s+l-2m},$$

where the summation s runs from $\max\{0, [m - (l-1)/2]\} \sim \min\{k, m\}$.

We remark that $2s + l - 2m = 2s + n - 2k$ and $2k + 2l - 2m = 2m + 2n - 2k$. For example, we have

$$\langle z^2 (z \cdot \alpha)^2, z^2 (z \cdot \beta)^2 \rangle = 4(p+4)(\alpha \cdot \beta)^2 + 4\alpha^2 \beta^2.$$

The variable p does not appear in the inner product if and only if $k = 0$ or $m = 0$. By using computers, we verified the above equality for small values of k, l, m, n.

Finally we give tables of the generators of lower irreducible components of $\mathcal{H}_n$ for $n \leq 5$. Note that the principal part of $\mathcal{H}_n$ coincides with that of S_n, and we omit them here.

$\mathcal{H}_2$: lower components
$\quad (0) \otimes V_2 : z^2$,
$\quad (0) \otimes V_{-2} : w^2$.

$\mathcal{H}_3$: lower components
$\quad (\Lambda_1) \otimes V_3 : z^2(z \cdot \alpha)$,
$\quad (\Lambda_1) \otimes V_1 : (p+1)z^2(w \cdot \alpha) - 2(z \cdot w)(z \cdot \alpha)$,
$\quad (\Lambda_1) \otimes V_{-1} : (p+1)w^2(z \cdot \alpha) - 2(z \cdot w)(w \cdot \alpha)$,
$\quad (\Lambda_1) \otimes V_{-3} : w^2(w \cdot \alpha)$.

$\mathcal{H}_4$: lower components
$\quad (2\Lambda_1) \otimes V_4 : z^2(z \cdot \alpha)^2$,
$\quad (2\Lambda_1) \otimes V_2 : (z \cdot \alpha)\{(p+2)z^2(w \cdot \alpha) - 2(z \cdot w)(z \cdot \alpha)\}$,
$\quad 2\,(2\Lambda_1) \otimes V_0 : (w \cdot \alpha)\{(p+2)z^2(w \cdot \alpha) - 4(z \cdot w)(z \cdot \alpha)\}$,
$\quad\quad\quad (z \cdot \alpha)\{(p+2)w^2(z \cdot \alpha) - 4(z \cdot w)(w \cdot \alpha)\}$,
$\quad (2\Lambda_1) \otimes V_{-2} : (w \cdot \alpha)\{(p+2)w^2(z \cdot \alpha) - 2(z \cdot w)(w \cdot \alpha)\}$,
$\quad (2\Lambda_1) \otimes V_{-4} : w^2(w \cdot \alpha)^2$,
$\quad (\Lambda_2) \otimes V_2 : z^2\{(z \cdot \alpha)(w \cdot \beta) - (z \cdot \beta)(w \cdot \alpha)\}$,
$\quad (\Lambda_2) \otimes V_{-2} : w^2\{(z \cdot \alpha)(w \cdot \beta) - (z \cdot \beta)(w \cdot \alpha)\}$,
$\quad (0) \otimes V_4 : (z^2)^2$,
$\quad (0) \otimes V_{-4} : (w^2)^2$.

$\mathcal{H}_5$: lower components
$\quad (3\Lambda_1) \otimes V_5 : z^2(z \cdot \alpha)^3$,
$\quad (3\Lambda_1) \otimes V_3 : (z \cdot \alpha)^2\{(p+3)z^2(w \cdot \alpha) - 2(z \cdot w)(z \cdot \alpha)\}$,
$\quad 2\,(3\Lambda_1) \otimes V_1 : (z \cdot \alpha)(w \cdot \alpha)\{(p+3)z^2(w \cdot \alpha) - 4(z \cdot w)(z \cdot \alpha)\}$,
$\quad\quad\quad (z \cdot \alpha)\{3z^2(w \cdot \alpha)^2 - 2w^2(z \cdot \alpha)^2\}$,
$\quad 2\,(3\Lambda_1) \otimes V_{-1} : (z \cdot \alpha)(w \cdot \alpha)\{(p+3)w^2(z \cdot \alpha) - 4(z \cdot w)(w \cdot \alpha)\}$,
$\quad\quad\quad (w \cdot \alpha)\{2z^2(w \cdot \alpha)^2 - 3w^2(z \cdot \alpha)^2\}$,
$\quad (3\Lambda_1) \otimes V_{-3} : (w \cdot \alpha)^2\{(p+3)w^2(z \cdot \alpha) - 2(z \cdot w)(w \cdot \alpha)\}$,
$\quad (3\Lambda_1) \otimes V_{-5} : w^2(w \cdot \alpha)^3$,
$\quad (\Lambda_1 + \Lambda_2) \otimes V_3 : z^2(z \cdot \alpha)\{(z \cdot \alpha)(w \cdot \beta) - (z \cdot \beta)(w \cdot \alpha)\}$,
$\quad (\Lambda_1 + \Lambda_2) \otimes V_1 : \{(z \cdot \alpha)(w \cdot \beta) - (z \cdot \beta)(w \cdot \alpha)\}\{(p+3)z^2(w \cdot \alpha) - 2(z \cdot w)(z \cdot \alpha)\}$,
$\quad (\Lambda_1 + \Lambda_2) \otimes V_{-1} : \{(z \cdot \alpha)(w \cdot \beta) - (z \cdot \beta)(w \cdot \alpha)\}\{(p+3)w^2(z \cdot \alpha) - 2(z \cdot w)(w \cdot \alpha)\}$,
$\quad (\Lambda_1 + \Lambda_2) \otimes V_{-3} : w^2(w \cdot \alpha)\{(z \cdot \alpha)(w \cdot \beta) - (z \cdot \beta)(w \cdot \alpha)\}$,
$\quad (\Lambda_1) \otimes V_5 : (z^2)^2(z \cdot \alpha)$,
$\quad (\Lambda_1) \otimes V_3 : z^2\{(p+3)z^2(w \cdot \alpha) - 4(z \cdot w)(z \cdot \alpha)\}$,
$\quad (\Lambda_1) \otimes V_{-3} : w^2\{(p+3)w^2(z \cdot \alpha) - 4(z \cdot w)(w \cdot \alpha)\}$,
$\quad (\Lambda_1) \otimes V_{-5} : (w^2)^2(w \cdot \alpha)$.

6. Reproducing Formulas of the Principal Part of Irreducible Subspaces of $\mathcal{H}_n$ for $n \leq 5$

In this section we give the reproducing formulas of the principal part of the irreducible subspaces of $\mathcal{H}_n$ on some orbits for $n \leq 5$.

In the following we denote by dh the Haar measure on $SO(p)$, and we put $e_j = {}^t(0\cdots 0\ \overset{j}{1}\ 0\cdots 0)$, $e_0 = e_1 + ie_2$. The following formulas on spherical harmonics are fundamental in our calculations.

Proposition 6.1 (cf. [3], [6], [12]). (1) *For any* $f_m \in H_m(\mathbf{C}^p)$, $g_n \in H_{n,p}$ *and any* $x \in S^{p-1}$, *it is valid that*

$$\delta_{n,m} f_m(x) = \dim H_{n,p} \int_{SO(p)} f_m(he_1) P_{n,p}(x \cdot he_1) dh,$$

$$\int_{SO(p)} f_m(he_1)\overline{g_n(he_1)} dh = 0 \quad (n \neq m).$$

(2) *Suppose f is continuous on the interval $[-1,1]$. Then for any $h_n \in H_{n,p}$ and any $x \in S^{p-1}$ we have*

$$\int_{SO(p)} f(x \cdot he_1) h_n(he_1) dh = \lambda h_n(x),$$

where

$$\lambda = \frac{\Gamma(\frac{p}{2})}{\sqrt{\pi}\,\Gamma(\frac{p-1}{2})} \int_{-1}^{1} f(t) P_{n,p}(t)(1-t^2)^{(p-3)/2} dt$$

(*Funk-Hecke formula*).

(3) *For $s, s_0 \in S^{p-1}$ the following formula is valid.*

$$\int_{SO(p)} (he_0 \cdot s)^n \overline{(he_0 \cdot s_0)^m} dh = \delta_{n,m} 2^n \lambda_{n,p} P_{n,p}(s \cdot s_0),$$

where $\lambda_{n,p} = \frac{n!\Gamma(p/2)}{2^n \Gamma(n+p/2)}$.

(4) *For any $f_n \in H_n(\mathbf{C}^p)$ and any $z \in \mathbf{C}^p$, it is valid that*

$$2^n \delta_{n,m} f_n(z) = \dim H_{n,p} \int_{SO(p)} f_n(he_0) \overline{(he_0 \cdot \bar{z})^m} dh.$$

Here, $P_{n,p}(t)$ denotes the Legendre polynomials of degree n and dimension p. For more details on spherical harmonics, see [3], [6], etc.

For $\widetilde{X} = \begin{pmatrix} 0 & X \\ {}^t X & 0 \end{pmatrix} \in \mathfrak{p}$ and $X = (x\ y)$ and $g = \operatorname{Ad} \begin{pmatrix} A & 0 \\ 0 & R(\theta) \end{pmatrix} \in K_{\mathbf{R}}$ ($A \in SO(p)$), where $R(\theta) = \begin{pmatrix} \cos\theta & -\sin\theta \\ \sin\theta & \cos\theta \end{pmatrix}$, we have

$$\Psi(g\widetilde{X}) = \begin{pmatrix} e^{-i\theta} Az \\ e^{i\theta} Aw \end{pmatrix}$$

and it is valid that for $f \in S(\mathfrak{p})$

$$\int_{K_{\mathbf{R}}} f(g\widetilde{X}_0) dg = \frac{1}{2\pi} \int_0^{2\pi} \int_{SO(p)} f \circ \Psi^{-1} \left(\begin{pmatrix} e^{-i\theta} h z_0 \\ e^{i\theta} h w_0 \end{pmatrix} \right) dh d\theta,$$

where $\widetilde{X}_0 = \Psi^{-1}\left(\begin{pmatrix} z_0 \\ w_0 \end{pmatrix}\right) \in \mathfrak{p}$. We put

$$\widetilde{E}_0 = \Psi^{-1}\left(\begin{pmatrix} e_1 + ie_2 \\ e_3 + ie_4 \end{pmatrix}\right), \quad \widetilde{E}_1 = \Psi^{-1}\left(\begin{pmatrix} e_1 + ie_2 \\ e_1 + ie_2 \end{pmatrix}\right).$$

Let $\alpha, \beta \in \mathbf{C}^p$ satisfy $\alpha^2 = \beta^2 = \alpha \cdot \beta = 0$. For $f \in \mathcal{H}_n$ we denote by $\langle f \rangle$ the subspace generated by the set $\{f(gX) \,;\, g \in K_{\mathbf{R}}\}$. In the following we identify $f \in \mathcal{H}_n$ and $f \circ \Psi^{-1} \in \mathcal{H}_n(\mathbf{C}^p)$.

Let $\widetilde{X} = \Psi^{-1}\left(\begin{pmatrix} z \\ w \end{pmatrix}\right), \widetilde{X}' = \Psi^{-1}\left(\begin{pmatrix} z' \\ w' \end{pmatrix}\right) \in \mathfrak{p}$. From Proposition 6.1 we have the following reproducing formulas on the principal part of irreducible subspaces of $\mathcal{H}_n$ ($n = 1 \sim 5$). We remark that all kernels $K_{n,k}$ in the examples below satisfy the equalities

$$K_{n,k}(\widetilde{X}, \widetilde{X}') = \overline{K_{n,k}(\widetilde{X}', \widetilde{X})} \qquad (\widetilde{X}, \widetilde{X}' \in \mathfrak{p}),$$
$$K_{n,k}(\widetilde{X}, \widetilde{X}') = K_{n,k}(g\widetilde{X}, g\widetilde{X}') \qquad (g \in K_{\mathbf{R}}).$$

Example 6.1 (cf. [10]).

For $k = 1, 2$ we put $\mathcal{H}_{1,k} = \langle (z \cdot \alpha)^{2-k}(w \cdot \alpha)^{k-1} \rangle$ and we put

$$K_{1,k}(\widetilde{X}, \widetilde{X}') = (z \cdot \overline{z}')^{2-k}(w \cdot \overline{w}')^{k-1}.$$

For any $g \in K_{\mathbf{R}}$, $K_{1,k}(\ , g\widetilde{E}_1) \in \mathcal{H}_{1,k}$ and we have the following reproducing formula of $\mathcal{H}_{1,k}$:

$$f(\widetilde{X}) = \frac{1}{2} \dim \mathcal{H}_{1,k} \int_{K_{\mathbf{R}}} f(g\widetilde{E}_1) K_{1,k}(\widetilde{X}, g\widetilde{E}_1) dg \quad (f \in \mathcal{H}_{1,k}). \tag{6.1}$$

Example 6.2 (cf. [10]).

(1) For $k = 1, 2, 3$ we put $\mathcal{H}_{2,k} = \langle (z \cdot \alpha)^{3-k}(w \cdot \alpha)^{k-1} \rangle$ and we put

$$K_{2,k}(\widetilde{X}, \widetilde{X}') = (z \cdot \overline{z}')^{3-k}(w \cdot \overline{w}')^{k-1}.$$

It is clear that $K_{2,k}(\ , g\widetilde{E}_1) \in \mathcal{H}_{2,k}$ for any $g \in K_{\mathbf{R}}$. Then we have the following reproducing formula:

$$f(\widetilde{X}) = \frac{1}{4} \dim \mathcal{H}_{2,k} \int_{K_{\mathbf{R}}} f(g\widetilde{E}_1) K_{2,k}(\widetilde{X}, g\widetilde{E}_1) dg \quad (f \in \mathcal{H}_{2,k}). \tag{6.2}$$

(2) We put $\mathcal{H}_{2,4} = \langle (z \cdot \alpha)(w \cdot \beta) - (z \cdot \beta)(w \cdot \alpha) \rangle$ and we define

$$K_{2,4}(\widetilde{X}, \widetilde{X}') = (z \cdot \overline{z}')(w \cdot \overline{w}') - (w \cdot \overline{z}')(z \cdot \overline{w}').$$

For any $g \in K_{\mathbf{R}}$ $K_{2,4}(\ ,g\widetilde{E}_0)$ belongs to $\mathcal{H}_{2,k}$. Then $K_{2,4}(\widetilde{X},\widetilde{X}')$ is the reproducing kernel of $\mathcal{H}_{2,4}$ and we have

$$f(\widetilde{X}) = \frac{1}{4} \dim \mathcal{H}_{2,4} \int_{K_{\mathbf{R}}} f(g\widetilde{E}_0) K_{2,4}(\widetilde{X}, g\widetilde{E}_0) dg. \qquad (6.3)$$

Example 6.3 (cf. [10]).

(1) For $k = 1, 2, 3, 4$ we put $\mathcal{H}_{3,k} = \langle (z \cdot \alpha)^{4-k} (w \cdot \alpha)^{k-1} \rangle$ and

$$K_{3,k}(\widetilde{X}, \widetilde{X}') = (z \cdot \overline{z}')^{4-k} (w \cdot \overline{w}')^{k-1}.$$

For any $\widetilde{X}' \in K_{\mathbf{R}} \widetilde{E}_1$ we have $K_{3,k}(\ ,\widetilde{X}') \in \mathcal{H}_{3,k}$. Then we have for any $f \in \mathcal{H}_{3,k}$

$$f(\widetilde{X}) = \frac{1}{8} \dim \mathcal{H}_{3,k} \int_{K_{\mathbf{R}}} f(g\widetilde{E}_1) K_{3,k}(\widetilde{X}, g\widetilde{E}_1) dg. \qquad (6.4)$$

(6.4) is the reproducing formula of $\mathcal{H}_{3,k}$.

(2) We put

$$\mathcal{H}_{3,5} = \langle (w \cdot \beta)(z \cdot \alpha)^2 - (z \cdot \alpha)(z \cdot \beta)(w \cdot \alpha) \rangle$$

and

$$\mathcal{H}_{3,6} = \langle (z \cdot \beta)(w \cdot \alpha)^2 - (w \cdot \alpha)(w \cdot \beta)(z \cdot \alpha) \rangle.$$

We define

$$K_{3,5}(\widetilde{X}, \widetilde{X}') = (w \cdot \overline{w}')(z \cdot \overline{z}')^2 - (z \cdot \overline{z}')(z \cdot \overline{w}')(w \cdot \overline{z}'),$$

$$K_{3,6}(\widetilde{X}, \widetilde{X}') = (z \cdot \overline{z}')(w \cdot \overline{w}')^2 - (w \cdot \overline{w}')(w \cdot \overline{z}')(z \cdot \overline{w}').$$

We can see that $K_{3,5}(\ ,g\widetilde{E}_0) \in \mathcal{H}_{3,5}$ and that $K_{3,6}(\ ,g\widetilde{E}_0) \in \mathcal{H}_{3,6}$ for any $g \in K_{\mathbf{R}}$. Then for any $f \in \mathcal{H}_{3,5}$ and $h \in \mathcal{H}_{3,6}$ we have

$$f(\widetilde{X}) = \frac{1}{8} \dim \mathcal{H}_{3,5} \int_{K_{\mathbf{R}}} f(g\widetilde{E}_0) K_{3,5}(\widetilde{X}, g\widetilde{E}_0) dg, \qquad (6.5)$$

$$h(\widetilde{X}) = \frac{1}{8} \dim \mathcal{H}_{3,6} \int_{K_{\mathbf{R}}} h(g\widetilde{E}_0) K_{3,6}(\widetilde{X}, g\widetilde{E}_0) dg. \qquad (6.6)$$

(6.5) and (6.6) are the reproducing formulas of $\mathcal{H}_{4,k}$ and $\mathcal{H}_{4,k}$, respectively.

Example 6.4 (cf. [10]).

(1) For $k = 1, 2, 3, 4, 5$ we put $\mathcal{H}_{4,k} = \langle (z \cdot \alpha)^{5-k} (w \cdot \alpha)^{k-1} \rangle$ and

$$K_{4,k}(\widetilde{X}, \widetilde{X}') = (z \cdot \overline{z}')^{5-k} (w \cdot \overline{w}')^{k-1}.$$

It is clear that $K_{4,k}(\ ,g\widetilde{E}_1) \in \mathcal{H}_{4,k}$ for any $g \in K_{\mathbf{R}}$. Then we have for any $f \in \mathcal{H}_{4,k}$

$$f(\widetilde{X}) = \frac{1}{16} \dim \mathcal{H}_{4,k} \int_{K_\mathbf{R}} f(g\widetilde{E}_1) K_{4,k}(\widetilde{X}, g\widetilde{E}_1) dg. \tag{6.7}$$

(6.7) is the reproducing formula of $\mathcal{H}_{4,k}$.

(2) We put

$$\mathcal{H}_{4,6} = \langle (z \cdot \alpha)^2 (z \cdot \beta)(w \cdot \beta) - (z \cdot \beta)^2 (z \cdot \alpha)(w \cdot \alpha) \rangle$$

and

$$\mathcal{H}_{4,8} = \langle (w \cdot \alpha)^2 (w \cdot \beta)(z \cdot \beta) - (w \cdot \beta)^2 (w \cdot \alpha)(z \cdot \alpha) \rangle.$$

We define

$$K_{4,6}(\widetilde{X}, \widetilde{X}') = (z \cdot \overline{w}')(z \cdot \overline{z}')^2 (w \cdot \overline{z}') - (w \cdot \overline{w}')(z \cdot \overline{z}')^3,$$

$$K_{4,8}(\widetilde{X}, \widetilde{X}') = (w \cdot \overline{z}')(w \cdot \overline{w}')^2 (z \cdot \overline{w}') - (z \cdot \overline{z}')(w \cdot \overline{w}')^3.$$

We can see that $K_{4,6}(\ , g\widetilde{E}_0) \in \mathcal{H}_{4,6}$ and that $K_{4,8}(\ , g\widetilde{E}_0) \in \mathcal{H}_{4,8}$ for any $g \in K_\mathbf{R}$. Then for any $f \in \mathcal{H}_{4,6}$ and $h \in \mathcal{H}_{4,8}$ we have the following reproducing formulas of $\mathcal{H}_{4,6}$ and $\mathcal{H}_{4,6}$.

$$f(\widetilde{X}) = \frac{1}{16} \dim \mathcal{H}_{4,6} \int_{K_\mathbf{R}} f(g\widetilde{E}_0) K_{4,6}(\widetilde{X}, g\widetilde{E}_0) dg, \tag{6.8}$$

$$h(\widetilde{X}) = \frac{1}{16} \dim \mathcal{H}_{4,8} \int_{K_\mathbf{R}} h(g\widetilde{E}_0) K_{4,8}(\widetilde{X}, g\widetilde{E}_0) dg. \tag{6.9}$$

(3) We put $\mathcal{H}_{4,7} = \langle (z \cdot \alpha)^2 (w \cdot \beta)^2 - (z \cdot \beta)^2 (w \cdot \alpha)^2 \rangle$ and we define

$$K_{4,7}(\widetilde{X}, \widetilde{X}') = (z \cdot \overline{z}')^2 (w \cdot \overline{w}')^2 - (z \cdot \overline{w}')^2 (w \cdot \overline{z}')^2.$$

It is clear that $K_{4,7}(\ , g\widetilde{E}_0) \in \mathcal{H}_{4,7}$ for any $g \in K_\mathbf{R}$. Then we have for any $f \in \mathcal{H}_{4,7}$

$$f(\widetilde{X}) = \frac{1}{16} \dim \mathcal{H}_{4,7} \int_{K_\mathbf{R}} f(g\widetilde{E}_0) K_{4,7}(\widetilde{X}, g\widetilde{E}_0) dg. \tag{6.10}$$

(6.10) is the reproducing formulas of $\mathcal{H}_{4,7}$.

(4) We put $\mathcal{H}_{4,9} = \langle \{(z \cdot \alpha)(w \cdot \beta) - (w \cdot \alpha)(z \cdot \beta)\}^2 \rangle$ and we define

$$K_{4,9}(\widetilde{X}, \widetilde{X}') = \{(z \cdot \overline{z}')(w \cdot \overline{w}') - (w \cdot \overline{z}')(z \cdot \overline{w}')\}^2.$$

It is clear that $K_{4,9}(\ , g\widetilde{E}_0) \in \mathcal{H}_{4,9}$ for any $g \in K_\mathbf{R}$. Then we have the following reproducing formula of $\mathcal{H}_{4,9}$:

$$f(\widetilde{X}) = \frac{1}{16} \dim \mathcal{H}_{4,9} \int_{K_\mathbf{R}} f(g\widetilde{E}_0) K_{4,9}(\widetilde{X}, g\widetilde{E}_0) dg. \tag{6.11}$$

Example 6.5

(1) For $k = 1, 2, 3, 4, 5, 6$ we put $\mathcal{H}_{5,k} = \langle (z \cdot \alpha)^{6-k}(w \cdot \alpha)^{k-1} \rangle$ and
$$K_{5,k}(\widetilde{X}, \widetilde{X}') = (z \cdot \overline{z}')^{6-k}(w \cdot \overline{w}')^{k-1}.$$

It is clear that $K_{5,k}(\ , g\widetilde{E}_1) \in \mathcal{H}_{5,k}$ for any $g \in K_{\mathbf{R}}$. Then we have for any $f \in \mathcal{H}_{5,k}$

$$f(\widetilde{X}) = \frac{1}{32} \dim \mathcal{H}_{5,k} \int_{K_{\mathbf{R}}} f(g\widetilde{E}_1) K_{5,k}(\widetilde{X}, g\widetilde{E}_1) dg. \tag{6.12}$$

(6.12) is the reproducing formula of $\mathcal{H}_{5,k}$.

(2) We put
$$\mathcal{H}_{5,7} = \langle (z \cdot \alpha)^4(w \cdot \alpha) - (z \cdot \alpha)^3(z \cdot \beta)(w \cdot \alpha) \rangle$$
and
$$\mathcal{H}_{5,10} = \langle (w \cdot \alpha)^4(z \cdot \alpha) - (w \cdot \alpha)^3(w \cdot \beta)(z \cdot \alpha) \rangle$$

We define
$$K_{5,7}(\widetilde{X}, \widetilde{X}') = (z \cdot \overline{w}')(z \cdot \overline{z}')^3(w \cdot \overline{z}') - (w \cdot \overline{w}')(z \cdot \overline{z}')^4,$$
$$K_{5,10}(\widetilde{X}, \widetilde{X}') = (w \cdot \overline{z}')(w \cdot \overline{w}')^3(z \cdot \overline{w}') - (z \cdot \overline{z}')(w \cdot \overline{w}')^4.$$

We can see that $K_{5,7}(\ , g\widetilde{E}_0) \in \mathcal{H}_{5,7}$ and that $K_{5,10}(\ , g\widetilde{E}_0) \in \mathcal{H}_{5,10}$ for any $g \in K_{\mathbf{R}}$. Then for any $f \in \mathcal{H}_{5,7}$ and $h \in \mathcal{H}_{5,10}$ we have the following reproducing formulas of $\mathcal{H}_{5,7}$ and $\mathcal{H}_{5,10}$.

$$f(\widetilde{X}) = \frac{1}{32} \dim \mathcal{H}_{5,7} \int_{K_{\mathbf{R}}} f(g\widetilde{E}_0) K_{5,7}(\widetilde{X}, g\widetilde{E}_0) dg, \tag{6.13}$$

$$h(\widetilde{X}) = \frac{1}{32} \dim \mathcal{H}_{5,10} \int_{K_{\mathbf{R}}} h(g\widetilde{E}_0) K_{5,10}(\widetilde{X}, g\widetilde{E}_0) dg. \tag{6.14}$$

(3) We put
$$\mathcal{H}_{5,8} = \langle (z \cdot \alpha)^2(w \cdot \alpha)\{(z \cdot \alpha)(w \cdot \beta) - (z \cdot \beta)(w \cdot \alpha)\} \rangle$$
and
$$\mathcal{H}_{5,9} = \langle (w \cdot \alpha)^2(z \cdot \alpha)\{(z \cdot \alpha)(w \cdot \beta) - (z \cdot \beta)(w \cdot \alpha)\} \rangle$$

We define
$$K_{5,8}(\widetilde{X}, \widetilde{X}') = 2(z \cdot \overline{w}')^2(z \cdot \overline{z}')(w \cdot \overline{z}')^2 - (w \cdot \overline{w}')(z \cdot \overline{z}')^2(w \cdot \overline{z}')(z \cdot \overline{w}')$$
$$- (z \cdot \overline{z}')^3(w \cdot \overline{w}')^2,$$

$$K_{5,9}(\widetilde{X}, \widetilde{X}') = 2(w \cdot \overline{z}')^2(w \cdot \overline{w}')(z \cdot \overline{w}')^2 - (z \cdot \overline{z}')(w \cdot \overline{w}')^2(z \cdot \overline{w}')(w \cdot \overline{z}')$$
$$- (w \cdot \overline{w}')^3(z \cdot \overline{z}')^2.$$

We can see that $K_{5,8}(\ ,g\widetilde{E}_0) \in \mathcal{H}_{5,8}$ and that $K_{5,9}(\ ,g\widetilde{E}_0) \in \mathcal{H}_{5,9}$ for any $g \in K_{\mathbf{R}}$. Then for any $f \in \mathcal{H}_{5,8}$ and $h \in \mathcal{H}_{5,9}$ we have the following reproducing formulas of $\mathcal{H}_{5,8}$ and $\mathcal{H}_{5,9}$.

$$f(\widetilde{X}) = \frac{1}{32} \dim \mathcal{H}_{5,8} \int_{K_{\mathbf{R}}} f(g\widetilde{E}_0) K_{5,8}(\widetilde{X}, g\widetilde{E}_0) dg, \tag{6.15}$$

$$h(\widetilde{X}) = \frac{1}{32} \dim \mathcal{H}_{5,9} \int_{K_{\mathbf{R}}} h(g\widetilde{E}_0) K_{5,9}(\widetilde{X}, g\widetilde{E}_0) dg. \tag{6.16}$$

(4) We put

$$\mathcal{H}_{5,11} = \langle (z \cdot \alpha)\{(z \cdot \alpha)(w \cdot \beta) - (z \cdot \beta)(w \cdot \alpha)\}^2 \rangle$$

and

$$\mathcal{H}_{5,12} = \langle (w \cdot \alpha)\{(z \cdot \alpha)(w \cdot \beta) - (z \cdot \beta)(w \cdot \alpha)\}^2 \rangle.$$

We define

$$K_{5,11}(\widetilde{X}, \widetilde{X}') = (z \cdot \overline{z}')\{(z \cdot \overline{z}')(w \cdot \overline{w}') - (z \cdot \overline{w}')(w \cdot \overline{z}')\}^2,$$

$$K_{5,12}(\widetilde{X}, \widetilde{X}') = (w \cdot \overline{w}')\{(w \cdot \overline{w}')(z \cdot \overline{z}') - (w \cdot \overline{z}')(z \cdot \overline{w}')\}^2.$$

We can see that $K_{5,11}(\ ,g\widetilde{E}_0) \in \mathcal{H}_{5,11}$ and that $K_{5,12}(\ ,g\widetilde{E}_0) \in \mathcal{H}_{5,12}$ for any $g \in K_{\mathbf{R}}$. Then for any $f \in \mathcal{H}_{5,11}$ and $h \in \mathcal{H}_{5,12}$ we have the following reproducing formulas of $\mathcal{H}_{5,11}$ and $\mathcal{H}_{5,12}$.

$$f(\widetilde{X}) = \frac{1}{32} \dim \mathcal{H}_{5,11} \int_{K_{\mathbf{R}}} f(g\widetilde{E}_0) K_{5,11}(\widetilde{X}, g\widetilde{E}_0) dg, \tag{6.17}$$

$$h(\widetilde{X}) = \frac{1}{32} \dim \mathcal{H}_{5,12} \int_{K_{\mathbf{R}}} h(g\widetilde{E}_0) K_{5,12}(\widetilde{X}, g\widetilde{E}_0) dg. \tag{6.18}$$

References

[1] C. DeConcini, D. Eisenbud, C. Procesi, Young diagrams and determinantal varieties, *Inv. Math.*, **56** (1980), 129–165.

[2] S. Helgason, Groups and Geometric Analysis, *Academic Press Inc.*, Orlando, 1984.

[3] K. Ii, On a Bargmann-type transform and a Hilbert space of holomorphic functions, *Tôhoku Math. J.*, **38** (1986), 57–69.

[4] K. Koike and I. Terada, Young-diagrammatic methods for the representation theory of the classical groups of type B_n, C_n, D_n, *J. Algebra*, **107** (1987), 466–511.

[5] B. Kostant and S. Rallis, Orbits and representations associated with symmetric spaces, *Amer. J. Math.*, **93** (1971), 753–809.

[6] C. Müller, Spherical Harmonics, *Lecture Notes in Math.*, **17** (1966), Springer-Verlag.

[7] M. Takeuchi, Modern Spherical Functions, *Translations of Mathematical Monographs* vol.**135**, Amer. Math. Soc., 1994.

[8] R. Wada, Explicit formulas for the reproducing kernels of the space of harmonic polynomials in the case of classical real rank 1, *Scientiae Mathematicae Japonicae*, **65** (2007), 384–406.

[9] R. Wada and Y. Agaoka, The reproducing kernels of the space of harmonic polynomials in the case of real rank 1, in "Microlocal Analysis and Complex Fourier Analysis" (Ed. T. Kawai, K. Fujita), 297–316, *World Scientific*, New Jersey (2002).

[10] R. Wada and Y. Agaoka, Some properties of harmonic polynomials in the case of $\mathfrak{so}(p,2)$, in "Legal Informatics, Economic Science and Mathematical Research" (Ed. M. Kitahara, C. Czerkawski), 81–88, *Kyushu University Press*, (2014).

[11] R. Wada and Y. Agaoka, On some properties of harmonic polynomials in the case of $\mathfrak{so}(p,2)$: Irreducible decomposition and integral formulas, in "New Solutions in Legal Informatics, Economic Sciences and Mathematics" (Ed. M. Kitahara, K. Okamura), 123–142, *Kyushu University Press*, (2015).

[12] R. Wada and M. Morimoto, A uniqueness set for the differential operator $\Delta_z + \lambda^2$, *Tokyo J. Math.*, **10** (1987), 93–105.

Contributors

Munenori KITAHARA, *Professor, Hiroshima Shudo University*

Munenori Kitahara (LL.M) is Professor of legal informatics (Rechtsinformatik) at the Faculty of Economic Sciences and the Graduate School of Economic Sciences in Hiroshima Shudo University, Japan. He lectures "Research on Information Society," "Legal Informatics," and "Personal Data Protection Management System." He was a guest professor at the Legal Informatics Institute of Hannover University in Germany (1999-2000).

He was a research member of legal expert systems (Legal Expert System Les-2, Lecture Note in Computer Science, No.264, Springer Verlag 1987). He is also a member of IVR. He presented several papers: "The Impact of the Computer on the Interpretation of Law (ARSP Beiheft 39, 1991), "Personal Data Processing and Business Ethics"(IVR 22nd World Congress, Granada, Spain 2005), "Ethics of Cyberspace: Information Ethics and Information Moral" (IVR 23rd World Congress, Krakow, Poland 2007), "The Right to Data Protection in Digital Society" (IVR 24th World Congress, Beijin, China 2009), "The Fusion of Law and Information Technology" and "Law and Technology Security Standard" (IVR 25th World Congress, Frankfurt am Main, Germany 2011), "The Information Society Law in Japan" (The 3rd International Seminar on Information Law 2010, Ionian University, Corfu, Greece). "The Information Society Law : The Fusion of Law and Information Technology" (The 5th International Conference on Information Law and Ethics 2012, Ionian University, Corfu). "Law and Technology: The Fusion of Law and Information Technology" and "Law and Technology: Legal Justice through Deploying Information Technology in Law" (IVR 26th World Congress, Belo Horizonte, Brazil 2013). He also published a paper titled "Legal Justice through the Fusion of Law and Information Technology" (*Legal Informatics, Economic Science and Mathematical Research*, Kyushu Univ. Press 2014). "Law and Technology: Regulations Compliance through Deploying Information Technology"(IVR 27th World Congress, Washington D.C. 2015).

His latest research is "Systematizing and Networking Information Society Law." The legal system consists of twelve legal groups and some fifty acts which have been related to information, information devices and information networks. He also proposes networking the legal system, and the fusion of law and information technology. He is researching on realizing a legal justice through using information technology.

Chris CZERKAWSKI, *Professor, Hiroshima Shudo University*

Professor of International Finance, Graduate School of Economic Sciences, Hiroshima Shudo University. Published in the area of International Capital Markets, Foreign Exchange Economics, Corporate Finance in journals in Japan, Australia and the USA.

Osamu KURIHARA, Professor, *Hiroshima Kokusai Gakuin University*

Osamu Kurihara was educated at Meiji Gakuin University, Hiroshima University and Hiroshima Shudo University, where he completed his PhD. He joined Hiroshima Kokusai Gakuin University as a Professor in 2006. He lectures Macroeconomics and International Economics in the University.

His research interests are Balance of Payments, Exchange rates and capital flows, currently and historically. He has been a director in Japan Academy for International Trade and Business from 2009.

Hiroaki TERAMOTO, *Hiroshima Shudo University*

He received his Master degree in Economics from Hitotsubashi University in 1972. Since 1989, he has been teaching Hiroshima Shudo University as a professor. His main teaching experiences include Modern Economics (1975~1997), Consumption Economics (1997~) at Hiroshima Shudo University. His special fields of study are consumer behavior and entrepreneur behavior. His major publications are as follows; "Productivity in Consumption — The Application of Household Production Function Approach—", Hitotsubashi Ronsou, 1986, Vol.95, No.5, pp.661-676; "Intergenerational Transfer of Income and Wealth", Keizai Kagaku Kenkyu, 1998, Vol.2, No.1, pp.91-112; "External Effects of Consumption and Economic Development", Keizai Kagaku Kenkyu, 2007, Vol.10, No.2, pp.39-56; "The Economic Analysis of Altruistic Consumer Behavior", in S. Hiraki and N. Chang (eds.), The New Viewpoints and New Solutions of Economic Sciences in the Information Society, Kyushu Univ. Press, 2011, pp.13-25.

Nan ZHANG, *Professor, Hiroshima Shudo University*

He is a professor of statistics in the Faculty of Economic Sciences. He received his Ph.D in Economics from Ritsumeikan University in 1993, has ever taught in Beijing University of Economics (1983-1989) and Peking University (1994-1995), and has been working in Hiroshima Shudo University since 1995. He has ever worked and working as visiting scholar in East Asian Institute at Columbia University (2001-2002), the Department of Statistics at University of California, Berkeley (2007-2008), and the Department of Statistics at Stanford University (2014-2015). He also has been named the Technical Assistance Expert by the Statistics Department of the IMF since 2008. His research focuses on Global Flow of Funds Analysis, Economic Statistics and Monetary & Financial Statistics. His major publications are as follows. The Flow of Funds Analysis in Theory and Practice: Statistical Observations on the Flow of Funds in China (Peking University Press, 2014); The Global Flow of Funds Analysis in Theory and Application (Minerva Shobo, 2005); The Basic and Application of Statistics (Chuokeizai-sha, Inc.,1999); and many papers published in such journals as Quantitative & Technical Economics, Statistical Research, Journal of Data Analysis, Statistics etc.

Setsuko SAKAI, *Professor, Hiroshima Shudo University*

Setsuko Sakai graduated from the Faculty of Education, Fukui University, 1979. She finished her doctoral course of Informatics and Mathematical Science at Osaka University in 1984. She became a lecturer at the College of Business Administration and Information Science, Koshien University, in 1986, and then an associate professor of the Faculty of Education, Fukui University, in 1990. Since 1998, she has been with the Faculty of Commercial Sciences of Hiroshima Shudo University, where she is a professor in the Department of Business Administration. She is currently working on game theory, decision making, fuzzy mathematical programming, optimization of fuzzy control by genetic algorithms and CAI. She is a member of the Operations Research Society of Japan, Japan Society for Fuzzy Theory and Intelligent Informatics, and the Japan Society for Production Management. She holds a D.Eng.degree. She has published papers such as "Tuning fuzzy control rules by α constrained method which solves constrained nonlinear optimization problems"(1999) and "Reducing the Number of Function Evaluations in Differential Evolution by Estimated Comparison Method using an Approximation Model with Low Accuracy"(2008) in The Transactions of the Institute of Electronics, Information and Communication Engineers, "Fast and Stable Constrained Optimization by the Constrained Differential Evolution", in Pacific Journal of Optimization (2009) and so on. She has also published papers in such journals as IEEE Transactions on Evolutionary Computation, Journal of Optimization Theory and its Applications, Transactions of the Japanese Society for Artificial Intelligence etc.

Tetsuyuki TAKAHAMA, *Professor, Hiroshima City University*

Tetsuyuki Takahama graduated from the Department of Electrical Engineering II, Kyoto University, in 1982. He finished his doctoral course in 1987. He became an assistant professor, and then a lecturer, at Fukui University in 1994. Since 1998, he has been with the Faculty of Information Science of Hiroshima City University, where he is an associate professor in the Department of Intelligent Systems. He is currently working on nonlinear optimization methods, learning of fuzzy control rules, machine learning, inference, CAI, and natural language processing. He is a member of the Information Processing Society of Japan, the Japan Society for Artificial Intelligence, the Japanese Society of Information and Systems in Education, the Association for Natural Language Processing and IEEE. He holds a D.Eng.degree. He has published papers such as "Structural Optimization by Genetic Algorithm with Degeneration (GAd)", in The Transactions of the Institute of Electronics, Information and Communication Engineers (2003), "Constrained Optimization by Applying the α Constrained Method to the Nonlinear Simplex Method with Mutations", in IEEE Transactions on Evolutionary Computation (2005), "Efficient Constrained Optimization by the Constrained Differential Evolution Using an Approximation Model with Low Accuracy", in Transactions of the Japanese Society for Artificial Intelligence (2009) and so on. He has also published papers in such journals as Information Processing Society of Japan Journal, International Journal of Innovative Computing, Information and Control Journal of Japan Society for Fuzzy Theory and Systems etc.

Ryoko WADA, *Professor, Hiroshima Shudo University*

Ryoko Wada is a Professor at the Faculty and Graduate School of Economic Sciences of Hiroshima Shudo University. She received the Doctor Degree of Science from Sophia University, Japan, in 1988. Her major research areas are harmonic analysis on homogeneous spaces. Especially she is engaged in topics on integral representations of harmonic polynomials. She also presented at a paper titled "Fantappié Transformations of Analytic Functionals on the Truncated Complex Sphere", M.Kitahara/K.Morioka (eds.), Social Systems Solutions by Legal Informatics, Economic Sciences and Computer Sciences, Kyushu Univ. Press (2010).

Yoshio AGAOKA, *Professor, Hiroshima University*

Yoshio Agaoka is a Professor at the Graduate School of Science of Hiroshima University. He graduated from Kyoto University (Faculty of Science) in 1977, and entered the Graduate School of Science, received the Doctor Degree of Science from Kyoto University in 1985. His major research areas are Differential Geometry, Representation Theory and Discrete Geometry. Especially he is engaged in topics on local isometric imbeddings of Riemannian symmetric spaces, decomposition formula of plethysms and classification of tilings of the two-dimensional sphere, etc. Recently, he is mainly engaged in the subject on elementary geometry from the viewpoint of classical invariant theory.

Series of Monographs of Contemporary Social Systems Solutions
Produced by
the Faculty of Economic Sciences, Hiroshima Shudo University

190 × 265 mm   5,000 yen (tax not included)

Volume 1   Social Systems Solutions by Legal Informatics, Economic Sciences and Computer Sciences

Edited by Munenori Kitahara and Kazunori Morioka   160 pages ISBN 978-4-7985-0011-9

Preface

Chapter 1 The Concept of Personal Data Protection in Information Society ⋯ *Munenori Kitahara*

Chapter 2 On the Evaluation System of Public Sector ⋯ *Kazunori Morioka*

Chapter 3 Effects of Property Right Restriction: An Analysis Using a Product Differentiation Model ⋯ *Koshiro Ota*

Chapter 4 Tax Coordination between Asymmetric Regions in a Repeated Game Setting ⋯ *Chikara Yamaguchi*

Chapter 5 The Household Production and Comsumer Behavior ⋯ *Hiroaki Teramoto*

Chapter 6 Modeling a Sequencing Problem for a Mixed-model Assembly Line ⋯ *Shusaku Hiraki, Hugejile and Zhuqi Xu*

Chapter 7 Long-run Superneutrality of Money in Japanese Economy ⋯ *Md. Jahanur Rahman*

Chapter 8 A Parametric Study on Estimated Comparison in Differential Evolution with Rough Approximation Model ⋯ *Setsuko Sakai and Tetsuyuki Takahama*

Chapter 9 Fantappié Transformations of Analytic Functionals on the Truncated Complex Sphere ⋯ *Ryoko Wada*

Volume 2   The New Viewpoints and New Solutions of Economic Sciences in the Information Society

Edited by Shusaku Hiraki and Nan Zhang   160 pages ISBN 978-4-7985-0055-3

Preface

Chapter 1 Economic Evaluation of the Recovery Process from a Great Disaster in Japan: The Case of Hanshin-Awaji Earthquake ⋯ *Toshihisa Toyoda*

Chapter 2 The Economic Analysis of Altruistic Consumer Behavior ⋯ *Hiroaki Teramoto*

Chapter 3 External Debt Default and Renegotiation Economics ⋯ *Chris Czerkawski*

Chapter 4 Statistical Observations on the External Flow of Funds between China and the U.S. ⋯ *Nan Zhang*

Chapter 5 Trade Flows in ASEAN plus Alpha ⋯ *Sithanonxay Suvannaphakdy and Toshihisa Toyoda*

Chapter 6 Inventory Policies Under Time-varying Demand ⋯ *Michinori Sakaguchi*

Chapter 7 RIDE: Differential Evolution with a Rotation-Invariant Crossover Operation for Nonlinear Optimization ⋯ *Setsuko Sakai and Tetsuyuki Takahama*

Chapter 8 The Network of Information Society Law ⋯ *Munenori Kitahara*

Chapter 9 The Function of the Copyright Mechanism: The Coordination of Interests of an Inventor and an Improver ⋯ *Koshiro Ota*

Volume 3 Social Systems Solutions Applied by Economic Sciences and Mathematical Solutions

Edited by Minenori Kitahara and Chris Czerkawski   156 pages ISBN 978-4-7985-0078-2

Preface

Chapter 1 The Collaboration of Law and InformationTechnology ⋯ *Munenori Kitahara*

Chapter 2 The Australian Broadband Policy: Theory and Reality ⋯ *Koshiro Ota*

Chapter 3 Evaluating the Impact of Mining Foreign Capital Inflows on the Lao Economy
⋯ *Phouphet Kyophilavong and Toshihisa Toyoda*

Chapter 4 Empirical Study of the Impact of the Thai Economy on the Lao Electricity Export
⋯ *Thongphet Lamphayphan, Chris Czerkawski and Toshihisa Toyoda*

Chapter 5 Calculating CO_2 Emissions for Coastal Shipping of Finished Cars by Pure Car Carriers in Japan ⋯ *Min Zhang, Shusaku Hiraki and Yoshiaki Ishihara*

Chapter 6 A Statistical Model for Global-Flow-of-Funds Analysis ⋯ *Nan Zhang*

Chapter 7 The Reproducing Kernels of the Space of Harmonic Polynomials ⋯ *Ryoko Wada*

Chapter 8 A Comparative Study on Neighborhood Structures for Speciation in Species-Based Differential Evolution ⋯ *Setsuko Sakai and Tetsuyuki Takahama*

Volume 4 Social Systems Solutions through Economic Sciences

Edited by Munenori Kitahara and Chris Czerkawski   156 pages ISBN 978-4-7985-0097-3

Preface

Chapter 1 Law and Technology: Privacy Protection through Technology ⋯ *Munenori Kitahara*

Chapter 2 The Signaling Role of Promotions in Japan ⋯ *Kazuaki Okamura*
—A Pseud-Panel Data Analysis

Chapter 3 The Chinese Spring Festival Model's Design and Application
⋯ *Gang Shi and Nan Zhang*

Chapter 4 Money and Real Output in Laos: An Econometric Analysis
⋯ *Inthiphone Xaiyavong and Chris Czerkawski*

Chapter 5 Literature Review on Ship Scheduling and Routing
⋯ *Min Zhang, Shusaku Hiraki and Yoshiaki Ishihara*

Chapter 6 Optimal Ordering Policies in a Multi-item Inventory Model
⋯ *Michinori Sakaguchi and Masanori Kodama*

Chapter 7 A Comparative Study on Graph-Based Speciation Methods for Species-Based Differential Evolution ⋯ *Setsuko Sakai and Tetsuyuki Takahama*

Chapter 8 Sino-Japanese Compounds ⋯ *Paul Jensen*

Volume 5 **Legal Informatics, Economic Science and Mathematical Research**
Edited by Munenori Kitahara and Chris Czerkawski   104 pages   ISBN 978-4-7985-0125-3

Preface

Chapter 1   Legal Justice through the Fusion of Law and Information Technology
··· *Munenori Kitahara*

Chapter 2   The Role of International Transportation in Trade and the Environment
··· *Takeshi Ogawa*

Chapter 3   A Comparative Study on Estimation Methods of Landscape Modality for Evolutionary Algorithms   ··· *Setsuko Sakai and Tetsuyuki Takahama*

Chapter 4   Some Properties of Harmonic Polynomials in the Case of $\mathfrak{so}\,(p, 2)$
··· *Ryoko Wada and Yoshio Agaoka*

Volume 6 **New Solutions in Legal Informatics, Economic Sciences and Mathematics**
Edited by Munenori Kitahara and Kazuaki Okamura   160 pages   ISBN 978-4-7985-0152-9

Preface

Chapter 1   Legality and Compliance through Deploying Information Technology
··· *Munenori Kitahara*

Chapter 2   Three-Good Ricardian Model with Joint Production: A Schematic Reconsideration
··· *Takeshi Ogawa*

Chapter 3   An Application of Cellular Automata to the Oligopolistic Market   ··· *Kouhei Iyori*

Chapter 4   Development of a Multi-Country Multi-Sectoral Model in International Dollars
··· *Takashi Yano and Hiroyuki Kosaka*

Chapter 5   Stochastic Inventory Model with Time-Varying Demand
··· *Michinori Sakaguchi and Masanori Kodama*

Chapter 6   A Study on Adaptive Parameter Control for Interactive Differential Evolution Using Pairwise Comparison   ··· *Setsuko Sakai and Tetsuyuki Takahama*

Chapter 7   On Some Properties of Harmonic Polynomials in the Case of $\mathfrak{so}\,(p, 2)$: Irreducible Decomposition and Integral Formulas   ··· *Ryoko Wada and Yoshio Agaoka*